UpRising

Surviving and Thriving in a World That Is Waking Up

Jen Madrone

GREEN HEART
LIVING
— PRESS —

ISBN Paperback: 978-1-954493-65-0

Published by Green Heart Living Press

This is a work of creative nonfiction. The events are portrayed to the best of the author's memory. While all the stories in this book are true, some names and identifying details have been changed to protect the privacy of the people involved.

For planet earth,
humanity,
and the next seven generations.

Contents

Introduction

When we think about spirituality or enlightenment, many people picture someone on top of a mountain in complete solitude, meditating in peace and communing with the Divine. Some may conjure up an image of a monk in a temple chanting mantras, or a shaman sitting in a cave in deep conversation with all of nature.

But this is not what modern spiritual awakening looks like. It usually looks a lot more like having an incredibly deep, mind–altering, metaphysical or spiritual experience and then having to get up the next day, make the sandwiches, drive the kids to school, and go to work, all while trying to act normal even though everything looks and feels completely different than it did yesterday and fighting the constant threat of massive tears (or hysterical laughter) coming to the surface in an uncontrollable eruption.

In this hectic, fast-paced age of overstimulation, ridiculous responsibilities, and constant input, many of us dream of being in a temple or a cave.

I would LOVE to be writing a book about the insights I gained while sitting on top of a mountain in deep meditation and in prayer with all of life. However, that's not what this book is about. It's about the messy, unexpected, chaotic, and deeply emotional process of modern awakening. It's about the bizarre experiences and symptoms that come with the spiritual awakening process, and it's about the incredible and massive transformation of us as individuals and as a planet.

The blessing (and curse) of modern awakening is that it matches the pace of the planet. As life has increased in volume, so has the speed of awakening. It's moving faster and faster every day, which is a blessing because it means that humanity is transforming more quickly than ever before, and it can feel a bit like a curse because it gives us so much to process all at once. This fast pace of modern awakening can leave you spinning—not sure if you are living or dying, awakening or losing your mind. The beautiful thing is that none of us are alone in this process. We are doing it together. We are healing and we are transforming—together.

This book is my attempt to put into words things and experiences that cannot be explained. Anytime we put words to indescribable experiences—we change it a little. I ask that you read this book with your heart, not your head, and that you feel into the energy behind the words and concepts being presented.

Speaking of words . . . I will be using some spiritual terms in this book that have countless meanings and connotations depending on your experience or background in the world of spirituality. I've found that one spiritual phrase or word can mean completely different things to different people. So again, I ask you to not get stuck on a single word but to sink into the energy behind it. Feel into what's true for you.

Throughout this book, I use many personal stories from my own experiences and from my clients and students who I have worked with over the past 20 years. Each story is deeply personal and is meant to relay or showcase various aspects of the awakening experience. It's my hope that they will deepen your understanding of certain concepts and show you that you are not alone in what you are experiencing—this is a collective experience we are having and it is impacting all of us whether we are undergoing an awakening or not. And, of course, the names of my clients have been changed to protect their privacy.

UpRising is intended to be a road map for places where there are no roads or paths. It's less of a self-help book and more of a survival guide, giving you the understanding and the tools to move through this life-changing process with as much grace, power, and awareness as possible.

However, there is a catch. The catch is that "you" will not survive the process of awakening. Who you think you are, the old you, the small you, is an illusion and will not make it through this process alive. However, the part of you that is eternal, the authentic you, is being simultaneously reborn and remembered, and "you" will never be the same.

There comes a time when staying asleep, closing our eyes to the truth, is no longer an option.
And then...
The painful process of transformation begins.
But beneath the pain, we feel the joy of beginning to see for the very first time.
Like a child who delights in everything around them.
This joy is what motivates us to move through the pain, to peel away the layers of illusion.
To rub our eyes and say:
"I am awake. Show me the truth."

Chapter 1

Revolution

It was a moment in time when the world stopped. I stood staring at my bare feet. The dirty sheets I was holding dropped to the floor and a powerful vibration moved through my body as I suddenly understood what was happening not just in my office, but in the world at large.

I had been seeing clients in my tiny but comfortable studio in Northern California. It was a cool day in the Fall of 2010. As I cleaned up the sheets and put away my supplies, I reflected on each person who had come in for massage and energy work that week. I was intrigued because most of them had one thing in common. They were all experiencing new and strange energetic sensations moving through their body, but their descriptions varied from person to person.

Some of these expressions included: electrical pulses, a sudden sensation of heat in isolated parts of the body, energetic shivers, an increase of frenetic energy that almost felt like a panic attack—but not quite, buzzing in the ears, a weird "tired but wired" feeling. Although the way they described it was unique to them, beneath the words they used was the same feeling of confusion mixed with curiosity and the notion that what they were experiencing was very different than anything they had felt before.

As I contemplated this, I began to realize that it wasn't just this week's clients who were reporting these strange symptoms. At that moment, I was hit with the realization that many of my clients over the past month or two or three had been showing up with similar symptoms. Whether they had originally come in for a stiff neck, a sore back, or a broken heart, a majority of them, often very apprehensively, shared these other things that had been happening to them. And then it hit me like a ton of bricks: these "symptoms," and many others they had reported, bore an incredible likeness to what I had gone through over the past couple of years.

Suddenly, the room closed in on me. My vision blurred. Outside noises drifted away and in that moment, there was only me, nothing else. As I processed this sudden epiphany, it all became clear. I was not the only one undergoing a deep spiritual earthquake. I had felt so alone and so strange, and absolutely crazy at times as I navigated what was happening to me and learned to live in a new reality. But in that moment, I realized that I wasn't alone, and it wasn't just a small group of people having these experiences. It was happening on a much larger scale than I could even imagine. I was being shown that this was a planetary event, not an isolated incident. This awakening was not limited to people in the spiritual realms or a freak act of nature; it was global, occurring in the undercurrent of life and holding the promise of changing the world. As I integrated this understanding, I was filled with excitement, hope, and a new resolve to assist in this process in any way that I can.

So You Think You're Special...

I have to admit that this realization was yet another powerful blow to my crumbling ego. There was a part of me that wanted to think that I was "special" for going through this incredibly deep and destructive spiritual transformation and that I was a part of an elite group of spiritual explorers, but with this realization came the understanding that it actually had nothing to do with "me." I was simply part of a much bigger transformation. I was just a grain of rice in this new landscape of spiritual evolution and my ego did not like that one bit.

Then again, you can't blame the ego. It's an opportunist and a shapeshifter. It will exploit any opportunity it gets to recover its power.

When our identity begins to fall away after an awakening experience, it's common for the ego to attempt to build a nicer, sexier, more attractive, and more spiritual identity around the fact that something big and important has happened to you, because it WAS big and it WAS important. However, it had nothing to do with how smart, spiritual, or special you are. It has everything to do with the fact that the energy on this planet is shifting, that we are experiencing a download of energy of a higher frequency causing our collective evolution to occur on the energetic and therefore spiritual level. We are all being affected.

The Hundredth Monkey Revisited

There was once a monkey on an island in Japan who grew tired of eating dirt with her potato every day. So she decided to take her potatoes to the river and wash them off before she ate them. The other monkeys watched and decided that this was a damn good idea so they followed suit, one by one, until every monkey in the tribe was washing their potatoes. However, things became more interesting when not only was the entire island washing their potatoes, but monkeys on the nearby islands, who couldn't have possibly observed this behavior, began washing their potatoes as well.

This iconic story[1] speaks of the ripple effect, or of a collective tipping point where once a certain idea, behavior, or energy has been replicated enough times, it directly changes the morphic field[2] around that behavior, allowing it to proliferate much more quickly than it has before. An otherwise unheard-of idea now becomes the norm.

As more and more people awaken to the truth of who they really are at the deepest level of their being, the foundation of humanity is shifting. From one perspective it looks like chaos—a complete falling apart of our political and social structures. It looks like genocide, abuse of power, war, manipulation, fear, violence, and poverty.

On the other hand, through the lens of awakening, it looks like all of the toxic behaviors, belief systems, dirty secrets, and outdated structures are coming to the surface and into the light of day. There, they can be seen, acknowledged, and burned to the ground. It is then

---

1. This story first appeared in 1979 in the book *Riptide* by Lyall Watson and was based on the findings of Japanese scientists studying macaque monkeys on the island of Kojima. Though the legitimacy of this study has been debated, the story remains a powerful analogy of a real-life phenomenon.

2. A morphic field is an energetic field of evolutionary information. It assists in organizing the bodies of plants and animals through vibratory patterns. For more information on morphic fields see the work of Rupert Sheldrake.

that they can be transmuted and transformed into something new that is in alignment with the new Earth that we are creating and that benefits all of humanity.

Unlike the horrific events we see in the media every day, we will not see this spiritual revolution unfold on any screen. This is truly an underground movement, an inside job organized only by the powerful, loving energies that move through our intelligent Universe.

We can see evidence of this global awakening if we look at popular culture. Practices like yoga, meditation, and breathwork have become wildly popular. Therapy and discussing childhood wounds, trauma, and even sexual abuse are much more accepted now than in the past. Also, working with sacred plant medicines such as Ayahuasca, Iboga, Peyote, and San Pedro has become much more accessible and sought after.

Even the more esoteric concepts such as past lives, psychic phenomena, channeling, card reading, and spirit guides are no longer taboo subjects. Many people are feeling inexplicably drawn to these topics and find themselves seeking out psychic readings and wanting to learn the ancient arts of tarot, divination, and channeling. The mainstream skepticism is falling away to be replaced by curiosity and intrigue fueled by a deep, innate desire for healing and self-discovery.

When I started to do this work so many years ago, very few people had ever heard the phrase "spiritual awakening." Even up until two or three years ago, many of my clients would express the fact that no one else understood what they were talking about. They would say it was difficult to find resources to explain what was happening to them. But now, spiritual awakening is almost mainstream; it is understood, and also very misunderstood, by many people. It has become a more common topic on social media, and even in movies and TV shows.

On one hand, this flooding of popular culture with spiritual concepts does water it down and even distort it a bit. There is a definite danger of losing the true essence and potency of the awakening experience as the phrase "spiritual awakening" gets thrown around loosely. On the other hand, the truth and power of these concepts are eternal and indestructible. They have no beginning, and therefore, can have no end. But just as more and more false or generalized information is being uploaded and downloaded, so too is the availability of perennial wisdom and ancient knowledge. True spirituality is there to be found by the sincere seeker.

I believe we have reached a critical mass in spiritual awakening. The morphic field of this spiritual revolution is growing and expanding every day. As each one of us finds the courage to walk through the fires of transformation and release the illusions that have kept us in suffering, the planet is changing. The old paradigm is being replaced. We are slowly tipping the scales. We are slowly lifting the veil, and we are beginning to remember who we really are. Your self-healing and self-growth are not selfish, they are essential to the healing of humanity and the healing of the planet. Awakening and listening to the truth of your soul allows others to do the same. **You are the hundredth monkey.**

Ancient Prophecies

For centuries, ancient cultures have been predicting this time of upheaval, change, and awakening. Indigenous nations have been prophesying about the disasters as well as the transformation that this current cycle of time has brought. The positioning of the planets and stars in our solar system and their relation to the Earth has created the perfect container for the extreme disruption of the toxic status quo. In this disruption, a new structure and new way of being and relating can be born. Our current-day astrology has also allowed for the flooding of the planet with ancient indigenous wisdom and secrets, as well as the downloading of transdimensional information and messages.

The Hopi of North America and the Q'eros elders of the Incan culture have similar prophecies that read, "When the eagle of the North and the condor of the South fly together, the Earth will awaken." This sacred prophecy speaks of a time of enormous change, or "pachacuti," which is a time when the world will be set "right side up" and peace and balance will be restored.[3]

The Toltec, Mexihca, Aztec, and Mayan cultures all speak of the time of the Sixth Sun and though the Aztec and Mayan calendars have some differences, they both illustrate the same thing—that we are currently transitioning from the time of the 5th Sun into the time of the 6th Sun.

The 5th Sun was a patriarchal sun, a time controlled by masculine forces. It was a "daytime sun" meaning that it was a time of looking outward for our answers. We are now transitioning into the 6th Sun, a matriarchal sun influenced heavily by the feminine. It is a "nighttime sun," a time of introspection, a time of looking within for our answers.

While the 5th sun was generally a more materialistic cycle in history, the 6th Sun is predicted to be a much more spiritual cycle of time.[4]

The precession of the equinoxes, or "The Great Cycle," observed and utilized in the an-

---

3. For more info on Hopi prophecies see *Book Of The Hopi* by Frank Waters. For more info on the Q'eros of Peru see *The Return Of The Inka* by Elizabeth Jenkins.

4. Sergio Magana, 2012-2021 *Dawn Of The Sixth Sun* and *The Real Toltec Prophecies.*

cient cultures of Egypt and Sumeria reflect similarities to the Aztec and Incan cycles.

Wisdom that was once kept hidden and protected in the mystery schools of the ancients is now coming to light. Ancient metaphysics, indigenous spiritual practices, and perennial wisdom are now being made available and accessible to everyone. This alone is enough to catalyze massive transformation, but coupled with the intense energetic shifts of the planet, personal and planetary awakening is inevitable.

What is Spiritual Awakening?

Spiritual awakening is the crumbling away of the lies, the attachments, the walls, and the limiting beliefs that have kept us separated from our true self. It's an extreme shift in consciousness, perception, and vibration. It's when we go from believing the illusion of the collective dream to seeing through that illusion and glimpsing the much bigger reality that encompasses us.

It's a vibrational event or shifting that causes us to question everything we think we know about who we are, what this world is about, and why we are here. We start looking deep within to find who and what we actually are.

It's about seeing through the veil of illusion and realizing that everything we believed to be true about ourselves and this planet and the world around us, is a lie. It's about releasing our attachment to our identity, to our beliefs, and to our reality as we know it.

No matter what we have read or the spiritual practices we have studied, the mind cannot comprehend it until the body has experienced it because it is not intellectual. It is deeply visceral and energetic, affecting us at the very core of our being.

Everything you believed to be true is now in question. You cannot be sure of anything—except for one thing and that ONE thing is the unshakeable LOVE bubbling up from the inside, the light we glimpsed as everything fell away. It's this LOVE that pushes us onward, it keeps us questioning and seeking the truth.

Awakening often creates a complete upheaval and total chaos in our lives. It causes a healing crisis as all of the traumas, conditioning, and old programs are shaken loose and begin to come to the surface to be healed and rewritten, and it's never what we expected.

It's completely different for each person because our unique awakening experience is based on our life circumstances and on what we came to the planet to learn, heal, and manifest. It is always the perfect storm of what we personally need to coax us out of our cave of comfort, force us to surrender our grip on reality as we know it, and release our attachment to what we believe to be true. That is the purpose of the awakening experience; to turn you upside down and shake you by one foot, and to pull the rug out from under your feet so that you can't go back to your old self and your old life even if you tried. It has to shift your reality so deeply that you don't believe it anymore.

Awakening is a process of deep remembering. It's waking up from a lifetime of amnesia because human life has a way of disconnecting us from our true selves and the gifts that we brought to this planet. We forget who we are below the surface of our occupations, our identities, our collection of experiences, and our traumas. As we begin to remember, we have to face the fact that we have created the illusion of a separate self—one that is disconnected from ourselves as the eternal, spiritual beings that we are.

Even though spiritual awakening is a very energetic, esoteric experience, there is also a very real physical component to it. The vibrational shift that creates an awakening shakes us literally to the bone, causing not only emotional and mental disruptions but also very real physiological disruptions. This sparks a detoxing process, clearing away years of trauma, pain and programming. The lower vibrations of our past lives have nowhere to hide. However, as we release we can begin to receive higher-level frequencies and downloads of new information as we reconnect with our original self.

Ultimately, awakening is the movement of living from the ego-centered mind, the separate self, and from the belief that we are only human—to living from the heart, the true self, and with the knowledge that we are not only human but also pure, multidimensional, eternal, spiritual beings. It's a process of healing, a process of self-love, and a process of deep surrender.

Awake Not Woke

There has been a new trend in society perpetuated by social media that speaks of being "woke." It's true that experiencing a spiritual awakening can cause us to be more compassionate, aware, and empathic, and has the capability to change social structures and heal outdated systems of power. But at its root, being awake is not political, religious, or hierarchical. It's much bigger than that. The term "woke" could be mistaken for the idea of awakening that I've described in this chapter. But being "woke" and being awake are very different things.

A Microcosm of the Macrocosm

We live in a fractal universe[5] where the personal reflects the planetary and the planetary reflects the personal. Nothing happens at the level of the cosmos that does not affect each of us individually.

At the same time, the deep personal work that each one of us does also has a profound effect on our planet as a whole. This is how important your individual healing and transformation are.

As more and more humans heal themselves and awaken to the truth of who and what they really are, we now have the power to heal our ecosystem, heal humanity, and change the world.

Just as there have been many planetary events that have sparked this global awakening, there are also countless events that can catapult us into our personal awakening process. It may be a very traumatic, life-shaking ordeal, or it may be a much more subtle alignment of energy that triggers awakening. However, when the time is right, the Universe will find a way to break us out of the trance of illusion.

---

5. A fractal is a repeating geometric pattern that forms the basis of creation. As the pattern is repeated, new forms emerge. At the quantum level, the same patterns can be seen in all of creation. The idea of a fractal universe has its basis in quantum physics as well as sacred geometry.

This awakening can feel like a free fall.
So fall.
You are falling out of the dream and into yourself.
And because you are pure love,
You will inevitably fall in love with yourself.
So fall.

CHAPTER 2

Signs and Symptoms

I'm not really a mall person. In fact, I dread entering a mall and subjecting myself to the bright fluorescent lights and strange semi-toxic smells. However, this particular Fall day, I found myself needing to visit one for some forgotten purpose.

Driving down the highway, assessing my inner state, and visualizing the errand before me, I began to laugh. As I compared my internal environment, which felt a bit like a psychedelic theme park, to the vision of middle America mall culture, I knew this trip had the potential to be a real shit show.

For several months I had been in an altered state of consciousness. My vision oscillated between normal 3D vision and a warping, transdimensional, extra sparkly vision that shifted and changed at its own surprising and not always convenient time.

I was experiencing a lot of electrical energy moving through my body in erratic patterns. I was feeling energized, electrified, and slightly insane. I had been struggling to hold it together and to appear "normal" and frankly I was surprised that more people didn't stop me to ask "What the hell is wrong with you?"

Pulling into the parking lot and walking in, I felt like I had just taken a large amount of LSD (even though that had not happened since my 20s and I preferred a very sober existence at this point in my life). However, as I awakened, it had become very normal for me to feel like I was permanently in an altered state of awareness, and being in the mall seemed to increase those feelings by a thousand.

My memory of the details is hazy, but I'm pretty sure I stood at the entrance with my mouth wide open for a period of time. I then left my body and watched with amusement as my trippy self tried to navigate this foreign environment. I watched as I struggled to find the words to ask for what I needed, locate the correct bills to pay for my purchase, and get the hell out of there as quickly as possible. I then made a solemn vow to myself to never, ever return.

A Vibrational Transformation

The symptoms of awakening can be very extreme, but they can also be much more subtle. They may begin before you even know that you are going through the awakening process or they may show up later, as the inner work begins and your shifting vibration starts to turn things upside down or inside out.

These symptoms appear on every level of your being and are a direct result of your change of consciousness and personal frequency. As you are downloaded with higher vibrational frequencies, energies that are at a lower vibration are no longer tolerated in the body and are pushed up and out so that they can be cleared. It is a deep spiritual detoxification process that occurs emotionally, physically, and energetically.

As we move through this detoxing process and as we integrate these new energies, it inevitably produces weird and challenging symptoms in our bodies. We are not only detoxing but we are also being reprogrammed and rewired back to our original, unique, and authentic form. These symptoms can be frightening, confusing, and vast but they are simultaneously clearing, cleansing, reprogramming, rewiring, and reconnecting you to your true self and to Spirit. This is the higher purpose for all of the painful, disorienting, challenging, and terrifying symptoms that we endure during the awakening process.

Mental/Emotional Symptoms

So let's start with the symptoms that have a profound effect on our mental and emotional states. These symptoms can be harder to identify than the physical/energetic symptoms or the metaphysical/spiritual symptoms because they are often more subtle and don't have an obvious physical, out-of-the-ordinary component. However, identifying and addressing these symptoms can help ease the intensity of awakening and help to heal long-standing personal issues.

Anxiety and Depression

"It feels like I'm having a panic attack but it's not quite like the normal panic attack" or "I feel depressed but it feels different than my old depression." These are words I hear often from clients as they enter or are already traversing their spiritual awakening. They often express feeling an increase in traditional mental/emotional issues such as depression, anxiety, and panic attacks but they always describe it as being a little bit different than the norm. When asked what the difference is, they may share an underlying optimism or peace, or just an innate knowing that this is part of something bigger and that it's going to be ok. This glimmer of hope may be small but it's this flavor that creates a different energy around these challenging events.

When these issues come as the result of an awakening, they feel different because the root cause is different. Before an awakening, these issues arise from our history of trauma and emotional wounding and from a feeling that we just cannot bear any more pain. The anxiety and depression are steeped in hopelessness, despair, and desperation. When a spiritual awakening occurs these symptoms appear as a result of the individual's shifting vibration.

The higher vibrational energies coming into the body push old, stagnant, and toxic energy to the surface. As these old energies emerge they can cause us to feel the uncomfortable sensations and emotions that originally created them. In both cases, these painful feelings are a result of unprocessed pain and trauma in the body that is looking for recognition and healing. When these feelings and issues surface, they are asking for acknowledgment, understanding, and unconditional love.

It can be essential at this point to get assistance with the healing process. Having someone to help you move through these feelings and shine a light in the darkness will allow you to move through this part of the process more quickly and with more grace and power.

There may be times that this anxiety and depression leave you feeling very lost, ungrounded, and as if you are out of control. It can make it very difficult to focus on everyday life and it may also create a high level of brain fog or disorientation. There may be times when it seems like you will feel this way forever but I promise you, you won't. As the energy continues to shift and move through you and as you stay present with what you are feeling and experiencing, the heaviness will lift, the fog will clear and you will have a much greater sense of clarity and connection than ever before.

Loneliness

Loneliness is also an extremely common and purposeful symptom and is one that almost everyone reports having during this unfolding. The extreme changes that come with awakening can often result in us losing connection to loved ones. Divorce, separation, breakups, and losing friends and family members is fairly common during awakening because we are shifting and changing so quickly and so intensely that we can no longer connect in the ways that we used to. Family members may not be able to understand what we're going through. They may think that we're losing your mind because you're no longer acting in the ways that are familiar to them.

We may also find ourselves walking away from toxic relationships because we can no longer tolerate them. Although this is enough to cause loneliness, the type of loneliness that accompanies awakening is much deeper than that.

It is a loneliness that rumbles up from the core of your being and is not dependent on whether you have close relationships or people around you. You may have five kids, a partner, and a busy job but still feel a sense of unnerving loneliness that you've never felt before and this is a crucial part of the process.

This depth of loneliness comes when we start to see through the illusion of needing others to complete us and we realize that we truly only have ourselves. As we accept that we are all that we have and we sink into this realization we may then come to the knowing that we have no clue who we actually are. So if we are all we have, but we don't know who we are, then what?

This existential crisis creates this deep loneliness but also sets the foundation and motivation for doing the soul-searching and healing that is required to know ourselves on the deepest level. As this reconnection with ourselves begins, we may still have some loneliness, but we also often have a deep craving to be alone. We need this time alone and away from others to get to know who we are and to separate from the people, situations, and expectations that have created our life up until this point. Being alone gives us the space to reclaim our relationship with ourselves and to learn to love ourselves again.

Fear

As we begin to drop our attachment to relationships and our need to have other's approval to feel complete, we may find some deep fears arising. This may be the fear of judgment from others—especially family members and the people closest to us. We may be afraid that we will lose loved ones if we are honest about what we are going through. Or we may be afraid that they'll think that we're seriously crazy and try to hospitalize or medicate us simply because they don't know what is happening.

These fears may be founded. Proceeding with discernment and trusting your intuition is always important. However, these fears may also be, and often are, exaggerations of the mind and a way of masking the bigger fear of the unknown. If there is a story of dangers and disasters that have not happened yet and the story just keeps getting more complicated and intense, then you can be sure that it is merely a fabrication of your frightened ego. It is not truth.

We may also become fearful that we ARE actually going crazy or that something is seriously wrong with us. This is normal and yet another invention of the mind. While it IS important to rule out any medical issues or chemical or mental imbalances, most of the time this fear is simply a result of our rapid change of consciousness and perception. As we adjust to this expanded reality, these fears will subside.

Overactive Mind

It is also very common to feel a high level of mental confusion and inner chaos as a result of an overactive mind. However, it's not that our mind has become more active, it's just that we have begun to notice it more.

Before awakening, it's normal to have a mind that is always talking, judging, fixing, assessing, blaming, criticizing, complaining, and commenting. We become adept at ignoring it even though it's constantly affecting how we live our lives. Once we begin to awaken, our level of awareness increases, and we become intolerant of the incessant noise in our heads. However, this intolerance isn't enough to fix the habitual noise that we've grown so accustomed to. It takes time and a lot of work to deprogram the mind from complete anarchy and reprogram it back to a place of order, intention, and peace.

As we become aware of our thoughts and refuse to accept the old status quo of the mind we find that we have the power (and responsibility) to choose these thoughts consciously. This is the beginning of taming the mind and learning to use it as the tool it was meant to be. As Ram Das says "the mind is a wonderful servant but a terrible master." Awakening is the process of dethroning the mind and placing it in its original role as servant or secretary.

We'll talk more about taming the mind and shifting the power structure from head to heart in chapter five.

Grief

Another emotional aspect of awakening is the experience of a deep, often unexplainable grief. This feeling of deep grief may bubble up unexpectedly and we may find ourselves crying or just feeling a deep sadness and a sense of loss. This grief comes from many places.

As we transform we must grieve the loss of our old self and our old life. We often grieve the loss of family members and friends or the loss of our old goals and interests. This grieving is an essential part of releasing our attachment to the past. It's important to allow ourselves time to grieve all of the old aspects of ourselves and to release them with love and gratitude.

Another aspect of grief that seems to run even deeper, is the grieving of the separation from ourselves. As we awaken and acknowledge how we have abandoned our true selves, we must grieve that separation in order to heal it. When we acknowledge the pain that we've caused ourselves, without judgment, we can then start the process of healing and reconnection. This is the highest frequency of unconditional love. Once we are able to access this frequency of compassion and love for ourselves we are then able to offer it to others.

Though all of these mental/emotional symptoms may feel very heavy and overwhelming at first, they serve to help us to actually lighten our load. When we lean into these symptoms and let them show us what we need to heal, we can then release a lifetime of buried pain.

On the flip side, you may also experience moments of profound peace, stillness, and clarity for no apparent reason. It may be fleeting or may last for days to months. These occurrences are the moments where the higher vibrational energy is breaking through and giving you a glimpse of where you are headed and what is possible. It is Spirit giving us the motivation to continue on and reminding us of why we are doing this in the first place.

Physical/Energetic Symptoms

A sweet, old friend contacted me because she had been experiencing intense heart palpitations for a couple of months. She had seen several doctors and specialists who had run all the tests but could find nothing physically wrong. When she tracked the timing of the beginning of these palpitations she wondered if there could possibly be a connection between the palpitations and the extreme internal transformation that she was experiencing. We worked together for a few months, diving into old emotional wounds, traumas, and childhood experiences. As we uncovered what was hiding in the shadows of her heart and fed her soul with love, the palpitations began to disappear.

The physical and energetic symptoms of awakening can be confusing, disorienting, frightening, and extremely varied. They may appear out of nowhere with no known reason or visible cause. Just like all of the symptoms of awakening, these physical symptoms are the result of shifting energy and our bodies attempt to adjust to and integrate these energies.

Exhaustion

The extreme shifts of energy often make us feel extremely exhausted and worn out even when we've gotten plenty of sleep. At the same time, because of the large amounts of energy moving through our bodies, we may have that "wired but tired feeling" or we may feel like we drank large amounts of caffeine when we haven't had any. It may be difficult to get out of bed and find the energy to get through the necessary demands of life.

This exhaustion is similar to the exhaustion you may experience when recovering from an illness or injury. It takes all of our physical energy and resources to heal that issue. It is the same with awakening. We are doing so much healing, processing, and internal shifting that it often takes all of our resources. Be gentle with yourself, allow the healing to happen, and know that your energy will return.

Aches and Pains

Experiencing weird aches or pains that appear out of nowhere or move around the body is also very common. Headaches, pressure in the head, digestive issues, heart pain or palpitations, and random mystery illnesses are fairly common during awakening. Though these mystery symptoms can be scary and cause us to worry about our health, they are doing a much bigger job.

These aches and pains are like a flashlight showing us where our energy blockages are located in our bodies. The pain and discomfort we feel is energy moving through the places where we have stored our old wounding, trauma, and fear. As the stagnant energy begins to move out, it often causes deep discomfort. It may move quickly, or it may take more time depending on the size of the blockage.

Approach these aches, pains, and illnesses with curiosity instead of fear. Breathe into them, ask them what they are trying to tell you, and let them move.

Electrical and Energetic Sensations

One of my favorite symptoms of awakening is the strange energetic sensations in the body. These may appear as tingling, buzzing, pulsing, or throbbing. They may also feel like intense electrical sensations that move around your body. There may be sensations of heat or cold in isolated areas.

These sensations are similar to what you may experience as energy releases while receiving energy work, acupuncture, sound healing, or other forms of alternative healing. However, they are often magnified and experienced in a much more intense way. They may come and go randomly or be a part of your reality for an extended period of time. It is a form of energy release and rewiring of the body.

Ringing or buzzing in the ears (that is not tinnitus) is also a fairly common symptom. When accompanied by awakening it is usually a much more pleasant experience and may be the auditory expression of the higher level energy that is coming in.

Involuntary Movements

I had another sweet client who came to see me when she was at the height of her awakening. She described the powerful involuntary movements that her body created during meditation, times of relaxation, or even sometimes randomly. Her body would begin to move on its own—swaying back and forth, head nodding up and down, or just violently shaking. Sure enough, every time we began the healing session with singing bowls or drumming, her body would begin to move. Many people report similar experiences of involuntary movement of the body. This is just another way that our intelligent bodies move energy through the system.

Metaphysical/Spiritual Symptoms

Years ago, in my online group, a woman who was going through an intense spiritual awakening shared an experience she had been having fairly regularly. She would be in her kitchen or folding laundry and would feel someone touch her on the shoulder. It was a very loving and gentle touch but when she turned to look, no one was there. After she shared her experience many other people began to share similar experiences of feeling a touch or a profound loving presence at times when there was no one else with them.

These types of experiences speak of the opening to other dimensions that is created after an awakening experience. In fact, it is really more of a reopening to the multidimensional world that we live in and a reminder of the multidimensional beings that we are. We are born fully aware of and existing in these various levels of reality. As we become indoctrinated

and domesticated, we are trained to see only
the three-dimensional reality—only the reality
that can be physically touched and logically explained. However, when this door opens again,
everything changes. The way we feel, the way
we see, the way we experience life is forever
changed.

During the awakening process, we experience this reality in a sometimes shocking way.
This is meant to make a deep impression so that
we are not able to go back to sleep or slip back
into the three-dimensional illusion.

Multi-Dimensional Sensory Experiences

The multi-dimensional world may show itself
through the touch or presence of a benevolent
spirit or ancestor or it may manifest in countless other ways. It is possible to have a change
in vision—from the typical 3D vision to a slightly blurred, sparkly, holographic 5D vision. You
may have flashes of past or parallel lives that
come up randomly, during meditation, or in
times of deep relaxation. You may begin to have
lucid dreams or you may even have experiences
like I had in the mall—feeling like you are in an
altered state of consciousness, living in a sort
of psychedelic reality. These multidimensional
symptoms are often much more intense in the
beginning or middle of an awakening and tend
to settle down once we have integrated and
accepted this new way of being and seeing.

Loss of Identity

Because of our shift in vibration and the shift back into a multidimensional reality, we often begin to lose our sense of identity. As our understanding of reality expands so does our understanding of ourselves. We no longer identify as just a mother, father, teacher, lawyer, artist, etc.

As we question who we really are we can no longer identify with the labels we acquire and we may feel like we have no identity at all. It is important at this point to not try to create a new identity even if it's a nicer, more beautiful, or more spiritual identity. Let yourself sit in that space of the void without attachment to an identity. It's in this space that you will begin to feel or experience who you really are beyond the roles and costumes that you have adopted.

As you sit in this void and the old identity falls away, it may bring up deep fears about death because a part of us IS actually dying. The fear of death may show up as paranoia about our health or sudden death, a fear of losing loved ones, or just a deep irrational fear of dying. We may also find ourselves simply obsessed with the idea of death and wanting to know what death really is. This is another very important part of the process. We'll talk more about it in chapter six.

Searching for Meaning

When our identity begins to slip away, it may also cause us to lose interest in the things that used to excite us or give our lives meaning. The things that used to hold great importance to us may start to lose their shine and significance. This can create an existential crisis that serves to push us into deeper soul-searching.

It's at this point that people often begin to have a strong desire to know their purpose and to live a more fulfilling life than the one they have been living. As they open to this possibility of a higher purpose, and search for deeper meaning, new gifts may emerge or old gifts that have been latent or under the surface may now begin to reappear. Many of my clients have told me about psychic, intuitive, or empathic gifts that they had as a child and lost that now begin to resurface as they awaken.

You may find new interests arising as your intuition and unique energy blueprint come back online. As your multidimensional self expands you may find that you are now developing a sixth sense, or that you have untapped gifts as a healer, artist, or psychic medium. Or it may be that your ability to truly love and accept yourself and everyone around you is your greatest gift. Whatever shows up for you, it is important to acknowledge these interests and gifts even if it feels confusing and frightening. It may be difficult to understand what is happening or what you are supposed to do with these gifts. Stay present but don't let them become your new identity. Instead, use them as tools to reconnect you back to your highest self and to show you how you can best serve humanity.

Managing and Channeling Symptoms for Your Highest Growth

The symptoms of awakening are not meant to be extra challenges or annoyances that we just have to tolerate in order to grow. They have a higher purpose and serve a very important part of the process. Each symptom shows us how energy is moving through our body, how we are changing, where the blockages are, and where we can focus in order to assist and speed up our growth and healing.

In general, the mental/emotional issues show us where our past trauma and wounds are, what our toxic programming looks like, and what the major internal issues are that our soul is asking us to heal in order to be free.

The physical/energetic symptoms show us where the energy blockages are in our body and assist us in the deep detox that is needed in order to clear those blockages out.

The metaphysical/spiritual issues serve to reconnect us with our multidimensional selves and to shake us out of a singular three-dimensional perspective.

All of these symptoms have the potential to be debilitating and they may increase in intensity until we give them the attention that they are asking for. We simply need to acknowledge them and experience them without fear or judgment and instead bring curiosity to their existence so we can hear what they are trying to tell us.

Pay attention to your triggers. Pay attention to the parts of your body that are asking for attention and use this information as the portal to take you deeper into yourself. These symptoms can be the catalyst for our shadow work because they are showing us the parts of ourselves that we have been avoiding and hiding from. It takes courage to face these shadows but often the intensity of our symptoms leave us with no other choice. We will go deeper into shadow work in chapter six.

In addition to using these symptoms for our healing and growth, it is also important to address them with deep self-care. During this part of the process, it's extremely important to nourish our nervous systems with plenty of rest, good food, moderate exercise, and any other self-care routines that you enjoy. A regular yoga, meditation, chi gong, or breathing practice can be extremely helpful. Be gentle with yourself. Take baths and long walks in nature. Know that it is not only ok but also very necessary to take lots of time to yourself so that you can process everything that you are experiencing. It is also vital to drink a lot of water during this time to assist in the physical and energetic detox process. You may find that you are very thirsty because of this.

When we are dealing with confusing and mysterious symptoms, it is important to rule out any medical or psychological issues. If you are unsure about the root cause of a symptom, be sure to seek the advice of a trusted medical or alternative healthcare professional.

Lastly, please keep in mind that you will not have all of these symptoms. You may only have a couple of them. This does not mean that you are doing it wrong or that you need to do more. Trust the process and know that it is unfolding exactly as it should.

Awakening—breaking open from the inside.
Like an earthquake that disturbs all things that
we thought were stable.
A deep internal disruption.
It cracks us open.
This time, the crack is not just where the light
comes in.
It is, rather, where our light,
which has been covered for so long,
can now shine out.

CHAPTER 3

Causes and Catalysts

Cadence, an incredible woman, client, and friend of mine, was born into the hands of a child abuser. She was raised in a religious cult and suffered severe physical, mental, emotional, sexual, and spiritual abuse. However, Cadence did not let these obstacles hold her down. As she grew, she found the courage to leave the cult which meant that she also lost the only family structure she had ever known. Years later, she married a man with whom she was deeply in love and they created a beautiful new family together. She thrived for years feeling supported and content in her life. However, in 2018 her young nephew committed suicide at the age of 13. Before leaving the earthly plane, he visited Cadence in spirit form as a beautiful macaw. In this form, he opened her heart and thus began her wild ride of awakening.

As she found herself in the cocoon of transformation, another tragedy struck. Her niece also chose to end her young life. This second devastating event was quickly followed by the earth-shaking realization that her husband, who she had completely trusted, was living a double life. His other life was sadistic, nefarious, and full of other women and other relationships. At this point, she dove into research mode, uncovering lie after lie and watching her beautiful life fall apart.

The culmination of these events created the perfect storm for a very deep and complete awakening. She found herself once again without any support structures at all, forcing her to lean into herself for the love and support that she needed. As she struggled to make sense of what was happening and to protect her children through this process, she found that a new strength was emerging. She simultaneously lost her marriage of 14 years and gained a relationship with herself that was beyond anything that she could have ever imagined.

As she stayed present with her physical reality, she also dove deeply into a new spiritual reality. She faced her shadows, sat in the discomfort, and slowly healed herself. During this time, her skills as a healer expanded exponentially and she stepped into her role as a conscious mother, gifted healer, and talented musician.

Cadence's story is a powerful example of how the most horrific experiences can create complete transformation. Her awakening experiences were exactly what she needed to bring her to her knees and surrender to Spirit and to herself. She is truly a warrior of the light and an endless inspiration.

There are so many ways that Spirit may use to crack us open and wake us up to the truth of who we are as limitless, conscious, and eternal spiritual beings. When the individual is "ready," the Universe will use any opportunity it can to open this door to awakening. I use the word "ready" very loosely because one, we can never really be "ready," and two, we may not even have any intention of getting "ready." However, this is a Soul-level experience, not a mental-level experience, so when the Soul is ready to level up, the Universe will respond in kind.

The process of spiritual awakening often begins with an experience like this that turns our life upside down and seems as if it's shaking you vigorously by one foot. After an awakening experience, we are often left with our mouths hanging open and our eyes wide, feeling completely blown apart. These experiences serve to pull the rug out from under your feet so quickly and so thoroughly that you can't go back to your old self, your old life, or your old illusions any longer. In essence, these are experiences that open the door for transformation and then it is up to us. We must decide whether we will walk through the door or not.

Keep in mind that most of the life-changing things on this list can be, and often are, experienced intensely, but they don't always trigger a spiritual awakening. The difference is in how it feels. When an awakening has been triggered there is a vibrational shift and often an influx or download of higher vibrational energy, something just feels very "different" internally, and is often accompanied by other symptoms of awakening. Even though there is usually a lot of stress at this time, there is also a heightened sense of optimism—a knowing that everything has changed and that you are stepping into something that feels more authentic than anything you have experienced before.

Awakening can be provoked by almost any experience. (I had someone in my online group report that her powerful awakening process was triggered by listening to a Tom Petty song.) It can also be a spontaneous occurrence that has no known impetus. However, there is often an event or series of events that breaks us out of our trance and places us on a completely different trajectory.

Here are some of the most common catalysts for the awakening process. Keep in mind that it is possible to have more than one awakening experience. We often have multiple experiences throughout our awakening process. Also, this is not a complete list. It is only a list of the more common ones, the possibilities are endless. When it is time, the Universe will find a way.

Divorce

Many years ago, in my mid-30s, I found myself spending many of my nights quietly crying on the bathroom floor trying not to wake anyone. Then in the morning I would get up, make breakfast, take care of the kids, and pretend like everything was fine. My marriage was falling apart and it felt as if my whole life was falling apart, too.

As my marriage crumbled, my belief in "reality" began to crumble as well. It was a perfect storm of spiritual seeking and personal crisis. I had been studying esoteric traditions, energy healing, and doing various spiritual practices. At the same time, my husband and I had grown very far apart. Our separation and divorce shook me to the core and was just one of the many experiences that catalyzed my awakening.

Above all others, divorce seems to be the most common catalyst for awakening that I've seen. When an intimate relationship ends we are often left feeling completely blown apart, questioning what has happened and how or if we can possibly recover from this.

Most intimate relationships, even the healthier and more loving ones, are very co-dependent in nature. This codependency only intensifies the feelings of extreme loss and desperation that we may feel when the relationship ends. We find ourselves suddenly all alone and the hole that is left from this loss often becomes flooded with all of our insecurities, fears, doubts, and traumas that we had been using the relationship to hide from. This overwhelming influx of feelings and the sudden crack in our reality is often the exact shift we need to open our eyes and push us into awakening.

The loss of co-dependency now opens the door for us to realize our true sovereignty, and to begin the journey back to ourselves. The emptiness that a divorce causes also creates a space for our true self to come flooding in.

When Alex was faced with divorce after 24 years of marriage, he was gutted, blown apart, and dealing with the deepest depression of his life. Feeling hopeless and with no other options, he began walking in nature every day as his only reprieve. One day as he reached the peak of the trail he experienced a deep, sudden, unshakeable peace and a very real understanding of what this life was about. In that moment, he not only began to heal from the pain of his divorce but he also began to reconnect with himself in a way that he never knew was possible.

Illness, Injuries, or NDEs

Many awakenings are catalyzed by the onset of an acute illness or an extreme injury that changes our ability to function normally and disrupts our everyday flow of life. Receiving a cancer diagnosis or becoming paralyzed by a car accident can serve to jolt us back into the present moment in such a jarring and terrifying way that makes everything else fade away. We are left only with ourselves and the reality of this fragile and temporary life.

This vulnerable state causes us to question our beliefs about our health, our bodies, and about being safe in these bodies. It often forces us to confront the reality of death in a whole new way and shows us the transient nature of life which causes us to search for something more.

A near-death experience (NDE), functions in a similar but slightly more dramatic and instantaneous way. An NDE is a temporary death or an experience of impending death. It separates us from this Earth-based reality and shows us what lies outside of this life's timeline. When someone experiences an NDE they can't unsee what they saw and they must reconcile this new understanding while living the life that they thought was over.

These types of experiences shake us to the very core of who we are and what we believe about ourselves. That shaking can be the exact thing that wakes us up.

Death of a Loved One

Years ago, I had a beautiful young client whose world was rocked by the sudden and traumatic death of her husband. She was left with four young children, a broken heart, and the chaos of entering into the awakening process unbidden. I was surprised by the amount of calmness she transmitted during our first call. She was so blown open by these experiences that she found herself with nothing left to do but to completely surrender control and allow Spirit to guide her.

When a loved one dies, the grief, shock, and emptiness that is felt, cracks open the doorway between dimensions. We are often given the unique experience of being in both the world of the living and the world of the dead (or ascended) at the same time. This experience can be a painful and potent launchpad for our awakening. The same is true for any form of sudden, shocking, or traumatic experience. Just like the example of Cadence's story, many people may face several deaths, traumas, and shocking experiences that create the perfect storm for transformation.

Depression, Psychic Splits and Mental Breakdowns

Eckhart Tolle was in an extreme state of depression and suicidal thinking when he had his awakening experience. He awoke one night in the midst of deep anxiety and fear, with the thought that he just couldn't live with himself anymore. This single thought spontaneously led to questions about who this "self" was and ultimately led to the dissolution of his small, man-made self. You can read more about him and his story in his brilliant book, *The Power of Now*.

Any sort of deep mental distress can be the perfect catalyst that causes us to sincerely question who we are and what this life is all about, especially when this mental distress is more emotional in nature rather than due to a chemical imbalance. Whether it is depression, extreme stress, a mental breakdown, or a temporary psychic split, the mind comes to a breaking point. Instead of, or in addition to, breaking down, it is also breaking open and allowing a new way of seeing yourself and the world to come flooding through. Unfortunately, this sort of awakening is often misdiagnosed as a medical or psychological emergency and is often treated with heavy medications or even by a visit to the psych ward, which can be extremely detrimental to the individual and to their process of transformation.

One example of this sort of awakening experience is illustrated in Sean Blackwell's book *Am I Bipolar or Waking Up?* In his book, Blackwell shares his fascinating story of finding himself in a state of complete ecstasy and bliss while participating in a self-help seminar. His sudden altered state resulted in the release of all of his inhibitions and so he quickly found himself in handcuffs, being arrested, and then promptly dropped off at the psych ward. The doctors diagnosed him with various mental disorders; a diagnosis that Blackwell immediately rejected. Instead, he embraced the transformation that had occurred and watched his life change in incredibly positive ways. He then dedicated himself to understanding what had happened to him and helping to educate others about this sort of spiritual awakening. I highly recommend you read his book for the rest of the story.

As this type of spiritual awakening becomes more common and more talked about, there are an increasing number of psychiatrists and doctors who are starting to understand the difference between a chemical imbalance and a spiritual awakening or spiritual emergency. It is my hope that books like this will help to educate professionals so that they are able to assist those going through this type of awakening in a way that serves their highest well-being and personal growth.

Spiritual Practices

As spirituality, yoga, meditation, and breathwork have become more mainstream, I have had clients who credit their awakening to listening to a guided meditation on YouTube, doing a particular yoga pose or session that activated their kundalini, or practicing mindfulness meditation or prayer. Their experiences are sometimes done with intention and sometimes done purely out of curiosity or boredom.

Either way, the effect was the same. They found themselves present with a spiritual practice and then everything changed.

When we are doing a spiritual practice we are aligning with a higher frequency which sets us up perfectly to receive a sudden shift in consciousness and vibration. Because of this perfect alignment, the awakening experience is often quickly followed by the presence of other awakening symptoms.

I have had other clients who were simply reading Rumi or listening to Alan Watts or Eckhart Tolle, but just like a spiritual practice, these readings placed them in the present moment with a higher vibrational energy.

Likewise, having a profound interaction with the beauty of nature can produce the same effect in the same way. I live in the redwoods and like many people here, I consider the forest to be my church. When I step into the trees the shift in energy is pure and profound. Whether your church is the forest, the ocean, the desert, the mountains, or the river, nature can be the perfect catalyst for your awakening.

Spiritual practices can also provoke slow gradual awakenings without a specific experience to point to. After devoting yourself to profound practices, introspection, and communing with the divine, you may find one day that you have profoundly changed and you are no longer the person you used to be. Over time, these spiritual practices have shifted the foundation for your life and created a new foundation of presence and peace. Though this sort of awakening still requires a lot of personal work and introspection, it is often (but not always) a gentler sort of awakening because it is slower and done with the strong intention of transformation.

Plant Medicine Experiences

After struggling with addiction for most of her life, Katya was at the end of her rope. Upon coming out of the psych ward and rehab, she was determined to stay clean, so she started to do some research. As she deepened her investigation, there was one word that caught her eye and then started to appear everywhere she looked. Ayahuasca. She was intrigued but had no idea how she would connect with this experience. It was 2014 and there was very little plant medicine being offered in the states, and especially in the Midwest, at that time.

About a year later she went to see a new doctor who was also an osteopath. After listening to her story, he asked her if she had ever heard of Ayahuasca. She perked right up. Now he had her attention. She expressed her interest in the medicine but also expressed her concerns about getting to Peru and having to come off of her pharmaceutical meds in order to work with it. He listened attentively and then the conversation shifted to a different topic. However, soon after the appointment, this amazing doctor contacted Katya to let her know about a shaman who would be holding an Ayahuasca ceremony nearby in the next few weeks. He offered to help her taper off of her meds that she was already cutting back on, she followed the recommended diet for 10 days and then they went to the ceremony together. When she got there, the Shaman told her that he would only give her a very small amount of Ayahuasca because she had not been off her meds for very long. She was disappointed but still grateful to be included in the ceremony. The obvious effects of the medicine were extremely minimal but the next day, Katya felt like a different person. Her depression had faded away, everything was sparkly and beautiful and she felt a new and extremely deep connection with nature. This was her introduction to Grandmother Ayahuasca.[1]

About a month later she returned for her second ceremony and this time she was able to take the full dose and have the full experience. The ancestors were singing and laughing and teasing her about her addictions. This ceremony cracked her open and cracked off a piece of her heavy exterior. She was a new person once

---

1. Ayahuasca is referred to as "Abuela" or "Grandmother" by the indigenous people of the Amazon. This title honors her as a teacher, healer, guide, and nurturer who can take a tough-love approach when needed.

again. She felt as if she was one with everything.

Her awakening had begun but there was still one more experience she needed to have to ensure her full transformation. Soon after her second Aya ceremony, her doctor friend told her about a man that he knew and trusted who would come to the house to offer private DMT ceremonies. She was all in. After smoking, she quickly left her body and saw God. She was everything and nothing at the same time. Toward the end of the session, she heard a voice sounding like a flight attendant who said, "You are at absolute zero." When she came back to consciousness she understood—everything. She saw clearly that we are all one, that life was simple and everything made sense to her. Her depression had lifted, her cravings disappeared and her awakening had fully begun. Katya often says, "There's my life before plant medicine and my life after. It's like night and day."

Plant medicines are healers of the heart and soul. They come from rich cultures that have carried these traditions for centuries for the health and well-being of their people. As the spiritual evolution of our planet quickens, these medicines have become more and more available to all of us because they are necessary for the transformation and healing of our Earth at this time.

Ayahuasca, Iboga, San Pedro, Peyote, DMT, mushrooms, LSD, and MDMA can be potent catalysts for the awakening process. They are also finally being recognized as powerful allies for mental health and emotional healing and some are now being welcomed into the therapeutic setting. They are masters at opening the doors of our consciousness and showing us what we need to see in order to heal old buried wounds and awake from the trance of suffering.

However, if you approach these medicines without preparation, without respect, and without someone experienced with these medicines guiding you and holding space for you, it can turn a potentially beautiful and transformative experience into a nightmare. These medicines are powerful and demand respect. If you feel the call to work with these potent allies—do your research, find someone who you connect with and who has extensive training in the medicine you wish to work with. Trust your intuition and know that the medicine will find you when it is time.

Twin Flame Experience

Amanda's marriage was failing. She had been doing some deep inner work and was struggling with the dichotomy of how her life was and how she wanted it to be. She was yearning for a deep spiritual connection and wanted to be seen for who she really was. At the same time, she met Matt, a man with whom she had felt an instant recognition, and their friendship began to grow. They had all of the same interests and could talk for hours, though it seemed as if only a few minutes had passed. They began to have experiences of shared past lives and other psychic phenomena. They could read each other's minds and feel each other's feelings even when they weren't together. Their deep emotional and romantic connection was undeniable.

Amanda had left her husband but Matt stayed in his marriage even though he continued to promise that he was leaving. As their connection intensified the web of lies also grew. Eventually, what started as a beautiful spiritual connection became a toxic love affair that exploded with incredible pain and betrayal. Amanda was left feeling completely shattered by the experience. She was deeply grieving and also struggling to deal with feelings of shame and guilt. At the same time, the energetic and psychic phenomenon that she experienced with Matt continued, but now it was completely self-contained—sparked in her alone and experienced only by her. These phenomena became the symptoms of her awakening process and as she worked to heal from this experience she found that she was also healing from the deep wounds of past and present lives that this connection had opened up for her.

Throughout her experience, Amanda felt like she was the only one who could have possibly experienced this level of depth, connection, and loss. Over time, however, she realized that she was not alone. She realized that what she experienced has also been experienced by many others and is a fairly common catalyst for the awakening process.

This sort of experience is often referred to as a twin flame experience although this term has contradicting definitions. It is a new-age term that refers to a strong spiritual, energetic, and intimate connection between two people. The contradiction comes in with what happens next after the connection has been made.

Some people believe that a twin flame is a more spiritually elevated version of a soulmate. Or that a twin flame is the other half of your soul or a "mirror soul." This definition is often exaggerated by the belief that once you find your twin flame, you must stay with them re-gardless of the circumstances. I've had clients who were told by other practitioners that they needed to stay with their twin flame even if the other person was toxic, married, or incapable of being in a healthy relationship. This definition only perpetuates the programming of codepen-dency which is in direct conflict with the inten-tion of spiritual awakening.

The other definition is that twin flames are merely catalysts for each other's growth. Even though this other person may feel like the one we've been waiting for our whole life, in actu-ality, they are simply serving to bring us back home to ourselves which is what we've actually been waiting and yearning for. The chaos and sense of loss that ensues after a twin flame encounter can make it easy to miss the opportunity for growth that is being offered. But in truth, it is a powerful invitation to stop searching outside of ourselves for the pure unconditional love and divine connection that we seek.

Getting Sober

From a young age, Sage had an innate knowledge of the presence of God, a higher power, or a universal energy. She remembers having long conversations with God while lying in bed at night. However, by the second grade, the painful experiences of life had worn her down and instead of talking with God in her bed, she attempted to take her life for the first time by holding her breath. Fortunately, she did not succeed.

As life progressed and intensified she began to seek ways to numb her sensitive spirit to the heavy, painful, and relentless realities that had now become "normal" life for her. Slowly this attempt at numbing turned into nightly drinking and blacking out. When she added Cannabis into the mix it brought up so much childhood trauma that she went deeper into alcohol and cocaine use to keep from feeling the pain. At the same time, her sister introduced her to yoga.

Eventually, her habit of driving drunk resulted in a D.U.I. and having her license suspended, but she hadn't hit rock bottom yet. Once her probation was over she began drinking again but also moved on to heavier substances. At the same time, she was falling in love. She moved to New York City with her new boyfriend who unbeknownst to her, was also a heroin addict. When she got to New York she began smoking crack and using more and more cocaine. She became obsessed with getting her boyfriend clean. She focused heavily on him and solving his problems instead of focusing on herself and her own issues.

She initially went to yoga because she loved the athletic aspect of it. She would go to class and hit the bar when she was done. However, her love for yoga had opened the door to the mystical and she found herself drawn to the esoteric teachings. As things in her personal life continued to unravel, she began to see the gravity of her situation. A desire and desperation to change things began to take hold. At the same, she started to study shamanism and breathwork. During an Ayahuasca ceremony Spirit told her, "All of the pain in your life has been because of the choices you have made." She began to make different choices. As her connection to herself and to the divine began to strengthen, her addiction entity dug its heels in and tried everything it could to bring her down. At this point, she knew she needed help. She turned to her sponsor in AA and was finally able to visualize a life without drugs and alcohol. She has now been clean and sober for seven years and lives an incredibly beautiful and powerful life as a healer, teacher, and spiritual leader. Sage's road to sobriety was the path that reconnected her with Spirit and with herself, which is ultimately the same thing.

Getting sober can be such a sharp and severe jolt to your consciousness that it can push you into another dimension and a new reality. This sudden shift is the perfect way to crack you open and to catalyze the awakening process.

Spontaneous Awakenings

This is a fairly rare form of awakening that I have only seen a couple of times. This is an awakening that happens suddenly without being sought after and with no known catalyst. When this occurs the person has not been seeking transformation, following any sort of spiritual path, or experiencing any of the above triggers.

I once worked with a woman who was living a very ordinary life. She was not a spiritual person and had never had a spiritual experience that she was aware of. She had a family, a job and the average amount of stress—nothing over the top. She described going to bed "normal" one night and waking up the next morning in an altered state of awareness. Her vision had become multi-dimensional, she was feeling unusual sensations in her body, and she expressed that she was just "seeing the world differently."

You may be thinking that this is the way to go and that it sounds like the perfect awakening. However, it can be just as traumatic as other awakening experiences because there is no preparation, no warning, and no tools to deal with what is happening. This kind of sudden, traumatic shift can be extremely terrifying, confusing, and discombobulating, to say the least. Someone who experiences this may also initially feel very angry because they just want their old life back. However, once they have accepted what is happening they are then faced with all of the same challenges that everyone else who is going through an awakening experiences. They must decide whether they are willing to do the soul-searching and deep healing work that is now surfacing for them.

An Awakening Event vs. the Awakening Process

An awakening event is the catalyst or wake-up call that is needed to begin the awakening process or to launch someone to the next level of their transformation. It is the first stage of the awakening process. We'll talk about all of the stages of awakening in the next chapter.

During an intense awakening event, we experience a much higher vibration than what we are used to. It feels amazing and powerful, but after a period of time it often begins to wane and we may begin to drop back towards the lower vibration that we felt prior to the initial experience. This is because it is now time to do the deep personal work that will allow us to sustain that higher vibration continuously. The best way to do this work is to learn to love yourself, every part of you, and though this may be easy to say it can be one of the hardest things you ever do and it's a process. When you learn to love yourself unconditionally, you will return to that higher frequency energy that you seek because love IS the highest vibration.

You are the portal.
You have the key.
You can choose to unlock the door and move
through.
Or you can choose to stay "safe."
The choice is yours alone.
There is no "should" or "supposed to."
No judgment.
There is only the whispering of your Soul—
Guiding you forward, shining the light,
opening the path,
asking you gently to surrender your fears,
to walk away from illusion,
and step into your Truth.

CHAPTER 4

The Anatomy of an Awakening

THE SEVEN PHASES AND STAGES OF SPIRITUAL AWAKENING

I have come to see the phases of awakening clearly because I have watched so many people work their way through them and I too have cycled through these stages many times in my life. However, it took me a few years to surrender to the call to name and describe the various phases of the Awakening process as I saw it. I was reluctant to write it up and put it out there as a linear progression for a couple of reasons. First of all, awakenings aren't exactly linear—they seem to defy time. Secondly, the process is different for everyone and it is possible to experience these stages in a different order or to find yourself in multiple stages at once. When I finally sat down and outlined the

basic flow that many Awakenings follow, however, it felt good to put a rough structure to
something that feels so amorphous while you're
going through it.

Since then, many people have expressed the
reassurance they have felt by reading through
these stages. As they identified with these
phases, they learned that what they are going
through is exactly that—just a necessary phase
that will change, they won't be stuck where
they are forever. It's my hope that this frame-
work will help you to see that you aren't going
crazy. There actually is a higher purpose and
plan to what you are experiencing.

The intention of this chapter is to give you a
basic layout of what to expect as you transform
and to help you clearly see where you are in
the process and where you are headed. You may
be able to easily identify yourself in a certain
phase, multiple phases, or somewhere in between. You may find yourself wanting to skip
past one stage to get to the next one. However, this is an organic process that cannot be
rushed. Each stage is vital to your healing and
growth and must be worked through thoroughly.

It is also possible to get stuck in a certain
phase because we are dreading the next one or
just don't know how to move forward. In this
case, we may need to push ourselves forward
or seek help and guidance with finding the next
step. As you read, hold these stages loosely

and know that as one cycle of transformation is coming to completion, another cycle is just getting started.

Phase One: The Wake-Up Call

The wake-up call is the very beginning of the awakening process. This is where life hands us an extreme experience that turns our reality upside down, cracks us open, and serves to abruptly change our experience and our perception of ourselves and of life in general. It is a complete jolt to our system. However, just as life as you know it begins to crumble, you are also getting a glimpse of another way. The internal earthquake that is produced by the wake-up call allows us to begin to see the truth of who we are more clearly.

This is the phase where we experience the various catalysts and causes that we discussed in chapter three. Usually, the catalyst IS the wake-up call that is needed to propel us into awakening. It may come as a product of spiritual seeking or spiritual practices, an NDE, a strong plant medicine or psychedelic experience, trauma, divorce, death of a loved one, illness, etc. It may also come spontaneously with no obvious reason. It may look like a bliss episode, a manic episode, a psychic split, or a period of samadhi, or it may not look like anything externally. However, internally, it feels like an inner explosion.

It is important to remember that regardless of our experience, this is just the beginning. If the wake-up call is a potent spiritual experience that leaves us in a state of complete bliss or offers us an experience of unity consciousness or samadhi, it can be easy to feel like we have arrived, we are done, and we have found enlightenment. Maybe we have found enlightenment for a moment or many moments, but we are definitely not done.

Early in my process of awakening and after a particularly powerful, extended breathwork practice, for the first time in my life I found myself in a very potent state of pure peace, complete presence, and a completely quiet mind-Samadhi. After being in this state for some time, I found myself thinking, *This is it, I think I've figured it out, I'm done.* With that one singular thought, my peace and presence came quickly crashing down because I was NOT done. I still had a lot of healing and inner work to do before I could sustain that level of presence or at least hold it for longer periods of time. Now that I had seen through the illusion of constant chaos and everyday reality, I knew where I wanted to be and now the real work began. I dove into the bottomless rabbit hole of awakening and moved into phase two.

Phase Two: The Rabbit Hole—Piercing the Illusion

Once we have seen beyond the veil of illusion, there's no going back. We do of course have free will so we could try to return to business as usual, but if we do, we will find that we are changed and that we cannot return to the person we were even if we tried. This is why the catalyst or wake-up call is usually such an intense life-altering experience. It has to shake us up so thoroughly that we can never find our way back to our old life again. This is the point in the process that we begin to realize that everything we thought to be true, is not actually true. We begin to see, feel, and know that what we previously believed about ourselves, about life and the nature of reality, is just an illusion. It may feel like a veil has been lifted from our consciousness and we are beginning to see for the first time.

As this veil of illusion between our seemingly three-dimensional life and the multidimensional world that we actually live in begins to lift, we may feel as if we have been lied to our entire lives. We begin to question everything we know to be true and start the search for a bigger truth. The wake-up call often gives us a glimpse of how life can be or how we were truly meant to feel. Then we have to do the work to find our way back.

This is a time of questioning EVERYTHING and it can feel extremely confusing, disorienting, and alarming. You may feel as if you are floating free, untethered to any particular reality. At the same time, a whole new multi-dimensional world is opening before your eyes. The recognition and exploration of the world beyond our limited three-dimensional reality becomes our inspiration and motivation to continue down this challenging and disorienting path. It is also this recognition that often opens us up to discovering new healing modalities and finding new tools for the expansion of our consciousness like meditation, breathwork, yoga or tarot. We may find ourselves going down a rabbit hole of new interests and exploring all things metaphysical, spiritual, and esoteric. This can be important food for our starving consciousness and often feels like a time of remembering because we are now reconnecting with lost parts of ourselves.

I have had multiple clients that have found themselves deep down in the rabbit hole of conspiracy theories and inhabited by a strong desire to uncover every single lie that was ever told on the personal, cultural, spiritual, and political level. They just wanted to know the truth! This desire to know the truth may look like an extreme pendulum swing away from the brainwashing of our culture and towards a completely different perspective. While this seeking can be a very therapeutic and necessary part of the process it is also important to not get lost in it. All of the questioning, seeking and research are tools to break us out of the trance, but they are just tools, they are not the path. We must eventually allow the pendulum to find the middle path of our own unique and grounded personal truth.

The rabbit hole of phase two is designed to be a force that pulls us into the very depths of ourselves. It is the beginning of the process of shedding the illusions of our ego, opening our minds and hearts, and releasing the conditioning of our culture as we begin the journey back home. It can be a time of great fear, confusion, and inner chaos, but it is also a time of wonderment, excitement, and inspiration as we glimpse beyond the veil to a new reality.

Phase Three: Separation and Isolation

As the sparkle and excitement of the wake-up call and the rabbit hole begin to wear off we may feel a heaviness beginning to settle in. The gravity of the powerful pull of the rabbit hole has now brought us deeply into ourselves. This is phase three.

At this point in the process, we often feel a very strong need to disconnect from the world around us in order to reconnect with ourselves. We begin to separate ourselves from our old life and from old friends, family members, and people in general. This may be an intentional decision, something that happens naturally, or it may feel like it is being forced on us due to events or situations in our lives. We may walk away from others or they may walk away from us. We begin spending more time alone and what once felt so familiar and comforting now feels foreign and off. Regardless of how it happens, this IS an essential part of the process. As we are undergoing major energetic and vibrational shifts, and processing our new reality, we must take time to ourselves to allow these changes to settle in.

As we extract ourselves from the world around us and find ourselves alone, possibly for the first time, we often begin to feel a deep loneliness, even though we may be craving this time alone. We may know at a deep visceral level that it is necessary. Feeling this extreme loneliness is very normal and often a very important part of the process. The experience of loneliness often marks the beginning of our shift from codependency to sovereignty. Until we are truly alone, we don't realize how we have used other people and the busyness of our daily lives to avoid feeling our deepest emotions and hearing what our hearts have been trying to tell us. This time alone is a gift. It gives us the space to hear what our spirit needs at this time and it offers us the time to learn the language of our Soul. This is the beginning of the healing process. We learn the value and power of being alone and we learn to care for ourselves in a whole new way.

However, hearing and feeling our deepest truths for the first time can be very intense, to say the least. The quietness we find ourselves in provides the space for us to feel the wounds of the past. We begin to become aware of our toxic habits, our outdated programming, and all of the ways that we mistreat ourselves. Being alone can also trigger old traumas around abandonment, betrayal, and neglect. As the ghosts of our past begin to surface and we are forced to face our deepest fears, we may find ourselves moving into phase four, the Dark Night of the Soul.

Phase Four: DNOS—Dark Night of the Soul

"The dark night of the soul comes
just before the revelation.
When everything is lost, and all seems darkness,
then comes the new life and all that is needed."
Joseph Campbell

When you find yourself in the deepest, darkest parts of your existence, face to face with all of the disowned and rejected parts of yourself, wrestling with your inner demons and feeling miles away from the light, this is the dark night of the soul. Even though you feel so far away, you are actually closer to the truth than you have ever been. Facing the darkness, stepping into the shadows, and embracing the parts of ourselves that we have abandoned is how we reconnect with our true self, with Spirit, and with our light.

The DNOS is the point of the process where the true work begins. Because of the massive energetic shifting that we have been through, we can no longer tolerate the outdated, toxic patterns that we have been holding onto up until this point. So we begin to feel all of the pain. We remember the traumas and everything that we have locked away in order to not have to feel it. It all comes to the surface so that we can feel it and heal it. This is a time when we are forced to deal with old wounding, outdated programming, and toxic beliefs. It may completely knock us off our feet while we heal. We begin to see and feel all of the ways that we have separated from ourselves and turned our back on ourselves. During this time, we are alchemizing more and more of our old trauma and pain that has kept us in suffering and operating from the ego as a defense mechanism.

As the DNOS settles in we may find ourselves having an "Oh shit" moment wondering "What have I gotten myself into?" It's usually at this point that we realize that spiritual awakening is nothing like we thought it would be, which is a good thing because if we knew what it was actually going to be like, we never would have made it this far into the process.

The DNOS may appear as an obvious by-product of our shifting vibration and our time spent in isolation or it may come as a result of a horrendous life event or circumstances that send us spiraling into the darkness. In either case, the purpose is the same—to bring us into contact with all of the barriers that we have built between us and love. It can be intensely emotional and feel very destructive as our old sense of identity continues to crumble, but it IS the work that your Soul has been waiting to do.

Phase Five: The Void—Spiritual Limbo

As we begin to come out of the DNOS we may feel a sense of relief and expect things to begin to open up and move forward in a new way. After a lot of hard work, we're ready for the light of divine inspiration.

However, what often happens is that we find ourselves in a place of stillness and stagnation. It may feel like the process has come to an abrupt and sudden halt after the rapid uprising of old energies, deep traumas, and the constant emergence of personal issues asking to be seen and healed. Now, after all of this work, things begin to slow down dramatically and almost stop.

We may wonder if we are doing something wrong. We may feel like we actually preferred the DNOS because at least things were moving.

And because of the sudden halt, we may also find ourselves asking if we are "making all of this up," wondering if everything we had just experienced was an illusion. This slowing down is an essential part of the process. It is a time of gestation. Though it may feel like nothing is happening, it is at this point that we are internally processing all of the incredibly deep work that we have done and are beginning to realign with our true selves. It is a powerful time of integration and a much-needed break but it can also feel very unnerving because it is in stark contrast to the rest of the awakening process.

During this time, we often have little to no motivation or inspiration and we might even feel like we are going backwards. This is because we have let go of so much of the old self but have not quite stepped into our true self. It is that limbo space between the old ego-centered self and the new authentic, heart-centered self. This transition takes time, which is why we often don't have a lot of motivation or inspiration.

Before awakening, most of our motivation came from the mind, the ego, and the thoughts of what we "should" do. Once we begin to awaken and move from ego to heart-centered living, that motivation is gone because it is no longer in alignment with our authentic self. This time period is about learning to move forward in a new way: with heart-centered inspiration, motivation, and action. It is completely different from how we were living.

This limbo space is essential in order to ensure that we don't go back to our old patterns, habits, and ways of moving through the world. At this point, we must allow ourselves to sit in the discomfort.

In the void, we learn to surrender to the unknown. It forces us to become okay with not knowing, which then creates space for Spirit to move through us as we reconnect. If you find yourself in this phase, allow yourself to be in the unknown, give yourself time to realign, and know that you are not doing anything wrong. Be patient, be gentle with yourself, and let yourself rest in the void. Giving ourselves time for this transition and integration is vital to our awakening process.

However, it is also possible to get stuck in the void. Once we have been in the deep entropy of this limbo space, the gravity of it can make it difficult to move forward. We may find ourselves knowing that it's time to move out of this phase but not having any idea of how to do that. This is when it can be very helpful to find someone who can help you get your footing in the heart-centered space and find your next aligned step in the process.

It's also very possible and normal to intuitively know when it is time to move on. We will often feel our life force returning and a new spark of light coming to the surface. This is the beginning of the rebirth.

Phase Six: Rebirth

The image of rebirth is very much like a seed that has begun to sprout after being buried deep in the dark ground, gestating, preparing and slowly opening to release new life. The tight seed is cracked open by the unstoppable force of life contained within that seed. The sprout then pushes to the surface guided by the most primal instinct there is—to seek light. And so it is with us. The awakening process strips away all that we are not and we become that seed, buried deep in the ground, gestating in the darkness and gathering our pure life force energy. This is our journey back to the light.

Up until this point we have been doing the work of reconnecting with ourselves, under the surface, in the fertile soil of the void. The rebirth happens once that reconnection has gained enough strength to move towards the surface. However, it is important to note here that we often have many cycles of DNOS into the void and then back into the DNOS followed by the void once again. This cycle continues as many times as is necessary in order to heal the pain that has kept us separated from ourselves.

Rebirth is a process of remembering who we really are at the deepest soul level and fully stepping into our power as eternal and spiri-

tual human beings. With this remembrance often comes the emergence of new gifts or of
old gifts that we had left behind or forgotten
about. These are often gifts of expanded consciousness that we suppressed in our childhood. They may be gifts of heightened intuition,
psychic skills, healing, or even artistic and mu-
sical gifts. The process of awakening has created the space and the safe container for these
gifts to come back up to the surface.

These new gifts may bring up a lot of excitement, fear, confusion, or overwhelm as we
struggle to understand and embrace them. We
may feel a deep fear of our own power or a
fear of judgment from others as we embrace
this new self. We may need help learning how
to develop these gifts in an authentic, skilled
way that can be of the highest service to those
around us. This rebirth may feel like it's happening very quickly or very slowly, and it usually
occurs in stages as we continue to grow and
uplevel.

Phase Seven: Re-entry

This is the point where we begin to interact
with the world around us and we step back
into our life with a new vision and a new way
of being. This interaction feels very different
from how we used to interact. It may feel very
strange and may take some time to get used to
being in public again.

The re-entry may feel a little rocky because we have never done it before and we must learn to move through the world and connect with others in a whole new way. Our deep reconnection now requires that we move from the heart and from intuition and truth rather than from ego or expectations. There is a learning curve here so be patient with yourself.

During rebirth and re-entry, we find that it's no longer an option to live our lives in the way that we used to. It is important that you move slowly and listen deeply to yourself and to Spirit, moving step by step as the heart leads you.

All of the work you have done has led you to this point and now you get to create and enjoy the beautiful and deeply authentic life that you have visualized for yourself, but stay vigilant. Be careful not to create a new ego around this new self and your new gifts.

As we begin to emerge from the intensity of Awakening we also intuitively know that the process never ends, it just deepens. As one cycle is completed, a new one begins. However, I've found that each cycle gets gentler over time. The first one is usually the one that really kicks us in the ass and gets our attention. After that, the work becomes more subtle and a bit easier because we now understand the process and have new tools to work with.

This is a process of true internal alchemy. We are transmuting the lead of our past pain into the pure gold of presence, authenticity, and personal power. Respect the process. Alchemy takes time and cannot be rushed. Know that you are being supported and led by the elements of nature, by the Universe, and by Spirit—every step of the way.

Sometimes the only way for Spirit to reach us
is to
burn
it
all
down.

CHAPTER 5

How to Die Before You Die

EGO DEATH DEMYSTIFIED AND THE FIVE LIVING DEATHS

On one beautiful, unsuspecting, June morning I woke up to do my breathing and meditation exercises just as I had been doing for the past 109 days. This was the same breathwork protocol that had produced the profound Samadhi experience that I described in chapter three and it was an exercise that was supposed to conclude at 104 days. However, I was eager to get back to that potent space of stillness so the gluttonous seeker in me kept going. On this morning, as I was completing the routine, I began to feel something intense moving through my body so I sat very still with my hands together at my heart, silently repeating the last word of the meditation over and over again. "Ometeotl"—duality transformed—a Nahuatl word that originates from the name of the Aztec god of duality. As I repeated this word, the energy I was experiencing grew to a dull roar and began to feel like a tornado moving through me. It quickly culminated into a forceful pulling sensation and felt as if something massive was being ripped off my back. I let out a loud exclamation of pain as it left my body. I then crumbled to the floor and cried for a very long time.

After this experience, I was unable to resume my normal life. I felt like I had died—literally. There was no spark of life force. There was no identification of self. I felt like the walking dead, and yet, the sun was rising and setting every day, the kids needed to go to school and I was still very much alive as I stumbled through life feeling like a zombie. After about two weeks of this, my beloved mentor at the time told me in no uncertain words that it was time to come back to the world of the living. With her help, I was able to locate my life force, find my footing, and emerge from the death zone—reborn. After that experience, I felt much lighter, much brighter, and much more empty. The dominant and urgent sense of self was now gone.

What is Egoic Death?

First, let's define the ego. The ego is our sense of identity. It is the small, transitory self and it lives in the mind. It's meant to be a tool to help us move through this human life, it is not meant to be in charge. However, once we started to believe the collective narrative that we are merely human and not spirit, we put the ego in charge and it took that power and ran with it. Awakening is the process of taking our power back from the ego, the small self, and returning it to our true self, our Soul.

The phrase ego death is a tricky one because it doesn't translate directly. The ego never completely dies. What dies is our attachment to our identity, to who we think we are, and the programming that has controlled us for so long. Egoic death is the metaphoric death of the false self. It's the act of releasing attachment to our identity. It's a gift but it is also a vibrational event. It occurs when the perfect storm of energetic upheaval culminates in support of your complete undoing, a total paradigm shift. This vibrational storm wakes up something deep inside. It opens you from the inside out. It is incredibly beautiful and devastatingly destructive at the same time. It is the transcendence or dissolution of our ego. It's putting the ego in its proper place as a tool—a servant of the heart. Even though the ego doesn't actually die, it's called ego death for a reason. It feels like an actual death because part of us IS dying—our old sense of identity and the illusion of the small and separate self.

The term ego death has been traced to many ancient spiritual traditions. Joseph Campbell defines ego death, within the context of the hero's journey, as a "complete loss of subjective self-identity, a phase of self-surrender and transition." It's a sub-process within the process of awakening, and just like awakening, there are various levels and intensities of ego death that we can experience. The experience I described above was an egoic death experience. Part of my ego, my identity, my sense of self, died that day and it was one of many small ego deaths that I have experienced throughout my life.

Ego-death experiences help us to begin the process of shedding the layers of illusion that have given the ego its power. Through the process of awakening, we go through many living deaths. Here are a few of the major deaths that we often experience.

The Five Living Deaths

One: The Death of Separation—Healing the Original Heartbreak

When we were born, we knew ourselves as pure spirit in human form, and up until a young age we remained very much connected to that spirit and lived completely from our heart. However, at some point the domestication sets in. We begin to believe the collective narrative that we are separate from Spirit and we are merely human (and usually a very faulty human). Essentially, we break up with ourselves and leave our true self behind. This begins as an unconscious protection mechanism to guard our vulnerable and pure spirit from the assault of the world. This misguided action leaves a huge hole in our heart and an incredible feeling of lack. This is the original heartbreak[1] —when we break up with ourselves as pure Spirit and let the ego take control. There may be a traumatic event in early childhood that causes this heartbreak or it may simply be the culmination of smaller events or the complete saturation of the collective programming.

This protection mechanism of separation may serve an important purpose for some time. However, we will eventually start to feel as if something very important is missing because it IS. Most of us attempt to fill this hole with external vices. We work, we exercise, and we adopt addictions like alcohol, drugs, food, sex, or TV. We use anything we can to fill the hole but there is always something missing. In order

---

1. The "original heartbreak" is a term given to me by my mentor Rebecca Haywood and it came to her through her work with Don Miguel Ruiz.

to find wholeness we must call bullshit on this illusion. We must find the courage to let go of the vices so we can take a deeper look.

Awakening is about smashing these illusions. Particularly, the illusion that we are separate from the spirit we were born with and separate from each other. As we awaken, we begin the process of healing the original heartbreak and reconnecting with the part of ourselves that has been in exile. Healing this heartbreak is a process of surrender and acceptance and it is usually characterized by a deep grief. This is often a sweet grief, like the grief of reconnecting with a long-lost friend or family member and there is also grief that comes with knowing that we hurt ourselves in this way. We must let ourselves feel that grief and then we have to forgive ourselves.

As we heal from this illusion of separation, we begin to experience our wholeness and our already-existent perfection. We blend the spiritual with the mundane and begin to see that it is all one. We have incarnated into these bodies to give our spirit a voice. There is, and can be, no separation. The anxiety and suffering that we experience come from the illusion that there is separation. The energy and force of will that it takes to maintain that illusion is exhausting and it goes against everything we know to be true at the deepest level.

If you are healing from the original heartbreak, feel the grief, forgive yourself, and be gentle with yourself. If you can trace this heart-break to a specific event, sit with the pain, and hold your inner child that experienced that event and give them love. If you can't pinpoint a specific memory, it's okay. You can still heal by focusing on the feeling of separation and calling back the part of yourself that you disowned. In either case, finding a gifted practitioner to walk you through the healing process can be vital. As you heal, allow for the blending of the mundane and the spiritual. You are already whole, com-plete, human, and eternal. You are perfect.

Two: The Death of Identity—Losing Ourselves to Find Ourselves

The other day, one of my students exclaimed-"I don't know who I am anymore. I used to think I knew who I was and now I have no idea!" This statement always brings joy to my heart. I love it when I hear someone say this because I know they are on the right path, they are letting go of the illusion of their identity and opening to the truth of who they are.

As we begin to see clearly through these il-lusions and gain the courage to really dig deep and search for our true nature, we start to come to the realization that we have no idea who we are. We begin to feel deeply that we have ab-solutely no clue who we really are without all of these illusions, identities, and programming. As we release our control and surrender our fears and attachments, we can finally admit that we don't really know what the truth is. At this point, we are closer to the truth than we have ever been. This is the beginner's mind—the clean slate. It's a beautiful thing. It is only from this place of emptiness that we can truly begin to experience ourselves.

Throughout our lives we collect a list of identities, beginning with our name given at birth and moving on to our role in the family as a son, daughter, brother, sister, etc. We collect titles and labels according to our occupations and interests. We may identify ourselves by the way we look, or by certain habits or characteristics. Our various identities make us feel like we have value, and something to contribute, and that makes us feel secure and safe. However, it also creates fear around losing those identities because if we do, we will lose our value and security.

When we begin to question who we are and we can no longer define ourselves as we used to, something interesting happens. We begin to feel like we are losing our grip on life. We often begin to feel like we are floating or free falling, untethered and ungrounded because our security was wrapped up in our outward identity and now that it is being questioned, we have nothing to tether ourselves to. This is perfect. In order to really know who we are at the deepest level we have to let go of the temporary identities. It's not that we stop being a daughter, dentist, or hippie. You are not losing these identities but you ARE losing your attachment to them. You begin to realize that these identities are not who you are. When you realize that you are not these things then you will be free from the fear of losing them.

It can be helpful to look at each identity as a costume that you are taking on and off throughout your day or throughout your life, but below the costume lies who and what you really are. The beautiful thing is that once we realize the deeper nature of who we are, then whatever we choose to do, we will be moving from a place of non-attachment and authenticity. Then whatever costume we choose to wear will be worn and done to the fullest, because we will be moving from a place of complete freedom and joy.

Three: The Death of Our Story—Healing Past Trauma

As humans, we often hold our stories and our personal history as sacred road maps that define how and why we are who we are. Holding our stories in this way can make us feel justified for being a certain way or for staying stuck in a certain pattern. We use our stories to explain to others about who we are and therefore we attach a large part of our identity to our stories. But even if we are able to let go of our attachment to our stories, they will still impact us.

The hardest and most traumatic experiences we have create emotional and energetic residuals that take up residence in the body. This is because a traumatic or dramatic event causes a very significant emotional response and this event imprints on our nervous systems. Then, weeks, months, or even years later, something in our environment triggers memories that are related to this past event and that triggers an emotional and chemical reaction in our body that matches our reaction to the original event. A pattern is created and each time the trauma is triggered, the pattern gets stronger. These stress chemicals from the lower emotions directly impact our nervous systems, our adrenals, and our immune systems. When we become used to and ultimately addicted to these chemicals, we are essentially locked into a stress response until we choose to change it. That is why we say "the issues are in your tissues" because your issue has just physically imprinted a learned response into your body.[2]

Since the issues are now in our tissues and because we become addicted to these chemical reactions, we also become attached to our stories, trauma, and wounding. We may begin to believe that our stories are who we are and we may begin to feel trapped by them. We may feel like we cannot change ourselves because we

---

2. For more info on this topic check out *Becoming Supernatural* by Joe Dispenza.

cannot change our history, but, in actuality, we CAN change our history. As we start to notice these triggers and the subsequent reactions, we can then choose a different response which will begin to break the cycle of addiction to these patterns. As we change our reaction to the triggers we can then change how we hold our story, we can change the way that they feel to us and we can change the way that we've been responding to them.

When we change our response and end the chemical reaction that we have to the event, we are changing our physiology, changing our energy fields, and clearing emotional toxins. Once we do this work, we are no longer controlled by these unconscious patterns and we are free to choose how we want to experience life.

These past traumas and issues often come to the surface during the awakening process so that we can clear our attachment to them. When these issues arise, it is your soul asking you to heal the past and move it out of your body. When we release attachment to our stories and traumas, we are making room for a new life and a new way of experiencing the world. This time we get to do it through heart-centered, conscious choice.

Four: The Death of Thought as Truth—Moving from Head to Heart

The mind is a blessing and a curse. When it is functioning as the incredible tool that it is, it can be brilliant, coming up with unique solutions and creative ideas. It helps us to move through our day, reminding us of the things we need to do and how we should do them. However, it also likes to dominate the present moment with constant, often meaningless, misguided, and self-destructive thoughts that we build our identity around. As we begin to reconnect with ourselves we must ask, "Is our relationship with ourself more of a relationship with our thoughts and with the endless conversation in our heads?"

When we are connected to our heart, the mind is brilliant, creative, intelligent, deep, expansive, and funny. It allows us to solve seemingly impossible problems and communicate our feelings, visions, and desires. But when we're living only in our minds and disconnected from our hearts, it becomes destructive, toxic, confusing, mean, abusive, judgmental, chaotic, and extremely misleading.

The problem is that before we awaken we believe that the mind is on our side. We believe that the voice in our head is our true voice, so we essentially believe everything we think. However, when we are disconnected from our hearts, that voice in the head is actually our out-of-balance ego running the show and it's not very good at it. The results of these beliefs are disastrous, often creating depression, massive anxiety, low self-esteem, inner confusion, low energy, and even violent or suicidal thoughts. Unfortunately, we get so used to living with this habitual negativity that we become used to it. It becomes background noise and we don't even know that it's there or what it's doing to us until it gets extremely loud and abusive or stops for a minute.

After we have had an awakening experience that interrupts the ego-centered mind, we may have a period of time where we are connected to the heart and the mind is relatively (or completely) quiet. However, when the mind becomes busy again, it often feels like it is much louder and more obnoxious than ever before. This is simple because we are now paying attention and once we have experienced its opposite we can no longer tolerate the noise and negativity.

Awakening gives us the motivation to question everything, especially our thoughts. When we begin to watch the mind from this new perspective, we are often horrified by what we see, and we should be. It is often the first time that we get a realistic view of what's going on behind the closed doors of our minds. At the same time, we are also beginning to hear the voice of our heart and this is what keeps us from going crazy. Even as we are hearing the out-of-control mind, our heart is speaking to us calmly and quietly, guiding us to question our every thought, and teaching us how to feel what is underneath the thoughts.

It's not an easy process. It often feels quite messy as we see the reality of our situation for the first time and begin to change it. We have to be brutally honest with ourselves and practice shifting our attention from the voice of the mind, the voice of the ego, and the voice of fear to the voice of our true self, the voice of the heart, and the voice of love.

As we make this shift from ego to heart and fear to love we begin to realize that our mind alone cannot be trusted and the death of thought as truth begins. This death, like all of the deaths, often feels like an actual death because we ARE losing what we thought was the foundation of our survival. We are NOT, however, losing our ability to think or use our mind. What we are losing is our trust in our thoughts and what we are gaining is learning to trust our hearts and learning to hear the voice of our intuition, our higher self. This process can be very challenging and discombobulating and it takes time and patience. We'll talk more about how to navigate this process in the next chapter.

Five: The Death of Loneliness—From Codependency to Sovereignty

When we broke up with ourselves during the original heartbreak, we locked away an important part of us and denied ourselves access to self-love. This is when the programming of not being enough began. We started to believe that we are not complete on our own and only the love and attention of others will make us feel complete. This creates a foundation for insecurity, disappointment, and codependency. When we feel unable to meet our own emotional needs and the people we depend on inevitably fail to meet our needs, a deep loneliness or longing is created. We seek others to complete us and to fill the hole we feel, but this belief and this seeking only sets us up for a lifetime of codependent relationships.

Most of our relationships, even the seemingly healthy ones, are codependent, meaning that we rely on the other person for something that we don't feel like we can provide for ourselves. When we are in codependent relationships, we are unconsciously (and sometimes consciously) sucking energy from each other and we still never feel fed or complete. The loneliness persists. But this loneliness that exists even when we are in loving relationships can often be the motivation we need to look deeper within ourselves to find what we are missing.

When we awaken we often go through a period of deep loneliness because we are finally letting ourselves feel what we have been pushing away for so long. We also feel this deep loneliness as we begin to go through the process of individuation because we must disconnect from these codependent relationships and from the people around us in order to reconnect with ourselves.

Individuation is the discovery of our wholeness, it is accepting ourselves completely and embracing our authenticity and it is a lifelong process. Often, while we are reconnecting with ourselves and finding our sovereignty as a human, we have to spend more time alone. We begin to learn that alone does not equal loneliness, just like loneliness does not equal alone. As we lose the need for codependent relationships and build a new intimate relationship with ourselves we are then able to have deeper relationships with others because we no longer need anything from them. Once we have connected with our true essence we begin to see this essence in others and we begin to experience the deep connection of all beings. This is true connection: when ALONE becomes ALL-ONE. It is miraculously beautiful.

This is the movement towards unity consciousness. When we truly discover the depth of who we are, when we discover ourselves as infinite spiritual beings, then we begin to see that essence in everything around us. The development of our inner strength, of our personal power and truly knowing ourselves is what unites us with others.

These five living deaths are just the beginning, there are many other deaths that we experience as we transform and we will often revisit parts of ourselves that we thought had died, only to discover that there is another layer. Stay vigilant and remember that there is no rebirth without death and we must allow for the little deaths that are seeking completion in every moment.

When we are seeking change, healing, or trying to manifest something new in our lives, we may not want to admit that something has to die and be released in order for this newness to come. It is the energy of what is dying, the transmutation of that belief system, insecurity, or relationship that provides the energy for the healing, change, or manifestation to happen. Our resistance to change is usually our resistance to death and our unwillingness to let go. For true transformation to occur we must surrender to death—over and over and over again.

It's a funny paradox that we must die in order to fully live. If you are going through a big death right now, surrender to the process and know that as the old dies the new is actively being birthed. It's not just about what is dying and being released—it's also about what is being revealed. As we strip away our blockages and barriers we can now see what was waiting underneath them. We can now connect with our truest self and highest love because there is no longer anything in the way.

If you are seeking change and growth, look for the little deaths and drop your attachments. As we learn to surrender to these continuous cycles, we learn the truth about death—it is not an ending, it is a beginning.

Awakening is not a straight shot.
It's a winding path,
Often spiraling back around again,
Giving us another opportunity to go deeper into
something we thought we had already healed.

CHAPTER 6

Spiritual Alchemy

THE LIVING ART OF AWAKENING

Alchemy: *The art of transformation; the process of moving from the primal state of unconsciousness into the evolved state of wholeness or enlightenment; the weaving of spirit and matter.*[1]

After being in the trenches of my awakening for many months, I was exhausted, worn out, and depleted. On this particular day, I found myself feeling immobilized by the exhaustion. I told myself a story about how I was extremely tired due to all of the deep personal work I'd been doing. Even as this story was playing through my head, a different image was forming.

In my mind's eye, I began to see myself running down a street with another version of myself following close behind, trying desperately

---

1. Nicki Scully, *Alchemical Healing*.

to catch up. In a split second, as I witnessed this scene, I realized that I had been running from myself (still) and this running was the source of my exhaustion. So I sat down on the curb, allowing the other version of me to catch up and sit down next to me. Then I took a deep breath. This was the first moment of true rest that I had gotten in a long time. I had finally stopped running away from myself and it was easier than you would think. It just took a moment of honest recognition and a willingness to do something about it.

Don't get me wrong, doing the healing, feeling, transmuting, shifting, and processing that is necessary during awakening IS exhausting. It requires a lot of energy and it is definitely a drain on our nervous system. However, we have to be careful to not hide behind the work, the doing, and the pain. At some point, we have to be very honest with ourselves so that we can see clearly what we've been missing or avoiding. For me, I had been running from myself and hiding in the painful minutia of my self-work. Even though I had been diving into the shadows and facing some big inner demons, I was still avoiding the most vulnerable and raw aspect of myself. Once I saw this clearly, I was able to let myself rest and acknowledge that the next step in my work was to be fully present with myself and with all of the messy, detached pieces of me. No more running.

The process of awakening is transformation at the highest level. It is true alchemy. Lead into gold. Darkness into light. Trauma into power. Classical alchemists were seeking the same sort of inner transformation and spiritual enlightenment, shrouded in the mysteries of their formulations and experiments. For the classical alchemist, the process of turning base metals into precious metals was an allegory for the transmutation of the base (lower) emotions and the chaos of the mind, into their pure essence—the alchemical gold of enlightenment. They knew this truth: that true transformation has to happen on every level.

Spiritual alchemy involves the same processes and it consumes all that you are. In many ways, the stages of awakening mirror the operations of classical alchemy very closely. As we move through the stages of awakening and the operations of spiritual alchemy we are directed and redirected towards the parts of ourselves that need to be thrown onto the alchemical fires. Over and over again, we are shown the deepest, darkest parts of ourselves that need to be worked with and brought into the light.

As we move through the transmutation of our blindness, our forgetfulness, and our programming we will come up against many pitfalls and distractions that threaten to throw us off the path. Here are some of the common pitfalls to keep an eye out for as you move through this process.

Pitfalls to Avoid

One of the biggest pitfalls or stumbling blocks that is easy to miss or to justify is **spiritual bypassing**. This is when we use our newfound spiritual interests, skills, or obsessions to distract us from the deep, painful inner work that needs to be done. We may throw ourselves into our yoga practice, reading tarot, working with plant medicine, or any other metaphysical endeavor because these things are much more fun and interesting than exploring our abandonment issues, addictions or traumas. It may also take the form of wanting to only talk about spiritual matters and judging others who can't meet us there.

Spiritual bypassing is the creation of a new ego—one that may be nicer, sexier, more spiritual, and possibly wears all white. This new ego will tell us that we are special and that we are different from the "others," which just feeds back into the old illusion of separation. Since this new ego is so different from your previous form and is often an upgrade in some sense, you may mistake this new ego for your true self, but it's not.

Our true self is still waiting for us beneath everything that we've been hiding from. When we start to source a new identity from our spiritual practices and tools, we need to stop, take a breath and remember that they are only tools.

Then we need to ask ourselves, what are the feelings or issues that lie beneath the surface? What is coming up for me right now that is uncomfortable or what is it that I am terrified to face? Answering these questions very honestly will help to get us back on track. We don't need to give up our practices and new interests, they are often a very important part of our healing and transformational journey. However, they are only meant to help us do the deep inner work, not be a substitute for it.

As we get further into our awakening process and begin to see that it actually looks nothing like we imagined, we may have a tendency towards **self-sabotage.** We may try to talk ourselves out of what we have experienced. We may begin to question if we are "good enough" to walk this path, or if all of this spiritual stuff is even real. We may even question our sanity and try to convince ourselves that we are mentally or physically ill. These are all brilliant techniques of the ego to disrupt the awakening process and protect itself. At the same time, we have been deeply conditioned to avoid difficult emotions and painful memories so it's very natural to have some resistance towards the grueling nature of this process. When we feel this resistance arising in us, it's important to be gentle with ourselves. Notice where it's coming from and ask yourself what you need in that moment. Be kind to yourself and know that as you move through each moment of resistance and self-sabotage, you are releasing the internal blockages and getting much closer to your true self.

Fear is another one of the biggest stumbling blocks to our path and is also one of the ego's favorite tools. Fear may appear in many forms and may change shape from moment to moment.

One of the biggest fears that comes up once we start to connect with our true nature is the fear of our own power. As we begin to connect with the immensity of our spirit and we see that we are so much more than just faulty humans, we may become overwhelmed by the possibilities of our power.

Glimpsing our own light and beauty can be completely overwhelming and fear-inducing. The idea that we are perfect, whole, and powerful is in complete contradiction to what we have believed most of our lives. Even once we've begun to accept the possibility of our perfection and begin to play with the idea of owning and expressing our inner beauty and ingenuity in the world, we are often confronted by life-threatening fear. What will happen if we speak our truth, if we own our gifts, if we set boundaries, and dare to offer viewpoints that are counter to popular opinion?

We fear the judgment of others. We become afraid of what our friends, family, and the world at large will think of us. There is also something deep in our DNA that goes beyond just our experience in this lifetime. We hold the memories of the visionaries, healers, and mystics who have been tortured and killed for being who they are, for expressing their truth, and for using their gifts. These memories become visceral and suddenly feel very real as we contemplate the possibility of allowing ourselves the true expression of our souls. As the layers of protection peel away, we are left feeling naked, vulnerable, and alone.

Despite these feelings, we are NOT alone. We have the support of those who have gone before us and who have paved the way for us. We have the support of our ancestors who are cheering us on and pushing us forward. Because the truth is that we are actually "safer" when we are vulnerable, authentic, and edgy because we are standing in our power and we are embodying the potent, limitless spirit that we are. This embodiment, this ownership, is why we are here. It's why we chose to incarnate on this planet—not to live in fear and self-doubt and to play small, but to bring our ineffable, eternal spirit to this life, to live in beauty, possibility, and pure love. You ARE that powerful and you ARE safe. We are blessed to live in a time where we will not be tortured, banished, drowned, or burned at the stake for speaking unpopular truths or sharing our psychic and healing capacities. So bring it. Bring your gifts, bring your beauty, bring your wacky ideas grounded in love, and watch what happens. As you move through your fear you will see the world around you expand and open to support you.

Your gifts are needed, your love is needed, and your power to transform light into dark is needed now. Don't deny the world of your gifts out of fear. Know that as you move forward despite your fear, you are breaking ancient patterns and destroying the collective programming. YOU are the one paving the way for the future visionaries who will follow in YOUR footsteps.

How the Ego Fights Back

As we move through these deep visceral fears and break down the barriers to our transformation, the ego will fight back every step of the way. In fact, it's only the ego that's created these fears in the first place. It's the ego that's created all of our protection mechanisms in an attempt to protect our sensitive souls from the world. When we were young these protection mechanisms were often necessary. However, at some point, once we have grown up a bit and the danger has passed, the ego shifts from protecting us to protecting itself. As we begin to question our beliefs and step into our power, the ego senses that it's losing its grip and it fights back in any and every way that it can.

The ego is the ultimate trickster. It knows how to hook our attention. It knows how to play the game. It will use our self-doubt, our self-pity, and our self-confidence to gain the upper hand. It will speak to us with harsh words or with words that justify our pain or suffering.

While we are going through the awakening process, the ego may tell us things like:

- "You're doing this wrong."

- "Are you sure you're not making all of this up?"

- "You're not spiritual, you're just crazy."

After we have done a certain amount of inner work and we have begun to see how the ego functions, it will change tactics.
It may start to say things like:

- "You've already done enough work. You've figured it out."

- "You don't need to meditate and do your daily practices. You're done. You can go back to your life now."

It's a shapeshifter, easily flowing from one form to the next, playing the ultimate head games and causing complete chaos and confusion in the process. This technique works perfectly for taking us out of our center, pulling us away from our true selves, and moving us out of our hearts and into our minds.

However, just like the trickster of Native American spirituality, it's also pointing us toward our healing and wholeness by showing us our triggers, our unresolved issues, and where we still have work to do. If we can detach from the ego, even just for a moment, and simply observe its misguided ways without judgment or reaction, we can learn so much about ourselves. We can see where our insecurities lie, we can see the traumas that still need healing, and we can see all of the ways that we have given our power away.

When we do this, we take our power back and begin to use the ego for our healing instead of letting it use us. Since the ego lives in the mind, we must take responsibility for every thought. If we want to take the controls away from the ego and hand them over to our true self we must stop feeding the ego and start feeding our essence.

Our ego feeds on thoughts of fear, insecurity, self-doubt, judgment, worry, and anger. Our authentic self feeds on love, beauty, kindness, compassion, peace, joy, curiosity and expansiveness. Don't be tricked. Instead, notice which one you're feeding unconsciously and then choose which one you would like to feed consciously.

It takes time and practice to become fully conscious of our thoughts and habitual patterns. It's a deep unlearning process and a complete reprogramming of the mind. Be patient with yourself but stay vigilant, and remember that when you take responsibility for your thoughts and allow yourself to become amused by the desperate antics of the ego, you will see its power quickly fall away.

Discerning Intuition from Ego

Many years ago I was driving down the road feeling happy and pretty good about life when a little voice crept into my head telling me that something was wrong with my young daughter who was currently away at summer camp. The feeling grew, but more than that, the story I was telling myself grew bigger and bigger and so did the fear. Five minutes later I was completely convinced that something terrible had happened to her, so I called the camp to find out how terrible it actually was. However, much to my relief, the cheerful voice on the other end of the phone told me that my daughter was just fine, and having a blast with her new friends. Of course, I was incredibly relieved but I was also very confused. How could my intuition lead me down such a dark and inaccurate path? Did this mean that I couldn't trust my intuition? No! Absolutely not. Because it was not my intuition that was speaking to me. It was actually the voice of my ego which felt very threatened by my happiness.

Due to the fact that the ego is a master trickster and shapeshifter, it can often masquerade as our intuition, hooking us at our point of weakness and reeling us in. The voice of fear can convince us that it's really our intuition speaking for our highest good, and it can be very, very convincing. Since then, I've had many clients who ask me how to discern between the voice of intuition and the voice of the ego. These are the four qualifiers I tell them to look for: 1) volume, 2) location, 3) quality, and 4) timing.

First, we notice the **volume** of the voice. When the ego is trying to hook our attention it is loud! It knows that because it's operating from illusion it needs to be the loudest voice in the room. It speaks at full volume and may even yell at us when it feels like it's necessary for its survival.

The voice of the intuition is quiet. It knows that it speaks truth so it doesn't need to be loud. It just is. It lives in the heart and holds a steady vibration of truth and love, waiting for us to clear the smoke and dust so that we can hear it. However, the voice of the intuition DOES have the ability to pierce through the noise when needed but it comes from a place of love and personal power not from a place of fear or desperation.

The second qualifier is **location**. The ego lives in the mind and the intuition or voice of our higher self, lives in the heart. Listen carefully and notice where the voice is coming from. You may feel contractions or other sensations in various places in your body depending on the memories and emotions it's bringing with it and what it's triggering in you. However, what we're looking for here is—where is that voice coming from? Where is it located? Do you hear it in the heart or the mind?

The next marker to look for is **quality**. The voice of the ego often feels desperate and sometimes quite aggressive because it's fueled by fear. It also has a way of rambling on and on, creating a huge, ever-changing story that supports its viewpoint. There may be several storylines being laid out to confuse and distract you from what you are truly feeling. The mind is relentless, never giving up or giving in, but the voice of the heart is succinct, precise, and to the point. Its messages are short and simple. There is no story or fear involved and it doesn't need to ramble on. It's consistent but not pushy. It's more feeling than thought.

The last tool of discernment is **timing**. The intuition shows up as the very first thought and there's a reason for this. Intuition lives in the heart, and the heart's electrical field is about 60 times greater in amplitude than the electrical field of the brain. It encompasses the whole body and because of its size, it's the first energy field to receive information and electrical impulses.[2] That information is immediately sent

2. For more information on this look into the Heart Math Institute.

to the brain for processing and so that very first thought is the most pure because it's coming straight from the heart. However, once that impulse or information reaches the brain, the mind grabs a hold of it and assigns meaning to it based on our past experiences, ingrained beliefs, or current mood. It is essential that we pay attention to that first thought before it gets corrupted. If we find that our mind has already gone on a rampage we can reel it in and work backwards to return to that first thought and find the origin point. Trust the first thought or first feeling—it IS pure intuition.

When you are trying to discern between head or heart, ego or intuition, love or fear ask yourself these questions:

- How loud or soft is the voice?

- Where is the voice speaking from?

- Is the voice telling a story or merely transmitting a message?

- Is the origin point close in time or farther away?

From Lead to Gold

As we break through all of the layers of the ego, let go of the illusions that support that ego, and release our meticulously curated protection mechanisms, we begin to see that we are the ones responsible for creating the life that we want to live.

Once we begin to take ownership of that responsibility and realize that that responsibility includes every aspect of our being—thoughts, words, actions, choices, etc.—we begin to comprehend the higher purpose behind all of the experiences that we've had to go through as we awakened. The truth is that the massive destruction and letting go that comes with the awakening and egoic death processes is not about torturing us until we finally give up and surrender, though that is often a side effect. It's ultimately about creating space.

In our sleeping life, before awakening, we had collected so many illusions, stories, traumas, and blocks that there was no space for anything else. We became hoarders of distraction, pain, and limiting beliefs. We were a well-guarded fortress against love, truth, beauty, and the infinite. The only way for Spirit to reach us was to burn it all down and clear it out, which is not always graceful but it IS effective.

Once we find ourselves emptied and cleansed by the fires of transformation, we can finally feel who we really are and we can hear the voice of truth once again. The emptying, purging, and detox process of spiritual alchemy, makes space for more love, more beauty, more creativity, and more authenticity than we ever thought possible. We must stay present with the process even when we are falling apart and remember that our breakdowns become breakthroughs on the other side.

As we take full responsibility for ourselves and move through this incredible process, we learn to harness the power of this often chaotic energy so that we can consciously use it for our own growth and self-mastery. This is how we turn lead into gold and it is beautiful!

Taking responsibility for this process means that we get to choose how we want to feel, what we want our life to look like, and how we respond to the triggers and challenges. Even though the awakening process never ends—there are always new ways that we can uplevel and life still has its challenges that can throw us off our center—we now have a conscious awareness of what is happening and an understanding of how we can work with what comes up.

We have tools, we have a greater acceptance and love for ourselves and we have a deeper compassion for others who are going through this crazy human experience, just like us. Life is no longer happening to us. We are now co-creating with life, with the Universe, and with Spirit. We are the alchemists. We are our own healers and gurus. We are powerful.

Awakening is not something you can do or check off the list.
It is an unfolding, a becoming, a dying and a rebirth.
It is stepping into the abyss,
not knowing if you will fall or if you will fly.

CHAPTER 7

Tools for Survival, Growth and Creating a New Reality

In January 2013, I found myself deep in the Amazonian jungle outside of Iquitos Peru. Through a series of synchronistic and magical events, I ended up at a traditional healing center to work with Ayahuasca—a powerful, psychedelic plant medicine used for centuries by the indigenous people of South America.

During the first ceremony, I was taken up to sit in front of one of the three Shipibo shamans who were leading the ceremony. As I sat in front of this powerful man, he began to sing an icaro, a traditional healing song sung in the native language, with deep intention. As he sang, I began to see this song as a river of green translucent light that gently flowed from his voice and into my body.

From my inner vision, I saw this green ribbon of light unscrew the top of my head which was then placed on the mat next to me. With that out of the way, the light of the song flowed gracefully through the crown of my head and into my body. As it filled my body, it illuminated the holes in my energy field- the places in myself that were traumatized, injured, forgotten or compromised. The song continued until every hole was healed and sealed with this green luminescence. Once I sensed that my body was full of light and all of the holes were repaired, the top of my head was put back in its place and the song was complete. This was just the beginning of the healing that I received that week.

A few days later, during my third ceremony after I drank my second cup of the bitter brew, I came to the realization that I must be dying. In my altered state, I was completely at peace with this fact. I remember feeling very grateful that my dear friend was with me so that she could tell my family what had happened to me. Once I accepted the idea of my own death, my body and any sense of myself completely disappeared and I found my consciousness in the cosmos—watching myself as a star that was dying and being reborn over and over and over again. This process of celestial death and rebirth continued for the rest of the night until I returned to Earth in my new form. I left the jungle a few days later as a new version of myself. Everything in nature was sparkling and full of light. The world was alive again and so was I. I felt lighter and happier but I wasn't entirely sure what had happened. It took many years before I could fully integrate the experience and understand the magic that had taken place.

As we awaken we often find ourselves opening to new ideas and experiences that we had previously been closed off to or never would have considered in a million years. We find ourselves gravitating towards people, places, and things that we instinctively know will help us with our healing and transformation and aid in the expansion of our consciousness. Having a variety of new tools, practices, and skills is essential to moving through this process with power and grace.

There are countless tools and modalities that can assist us in expanding our consciousness and opening our hearts, and plant medicine is just one of those tools. Meditation, yoga, breathwork, various forms of energy work, and sound healing are just a few of the very accessible practices that can keep us grounded, focused, and connected to Spirit as we navigate the challenges of awakening. In this chapter, we will dive into these various modalities and also discuss the importance of self-care and shadow work in the transformational process. As you build your toolbox and find the practices that lift you up, you will also be building a strong foundation for your continued growth and ongoing transformation.

More on Sacred Plant Medicine

Many years after my introduction to Ayahuasca, I was drawn to Iboga plant medicine, so I began to do some research. Tabernanthe Iboga is a rainforest plant native to Gabon, Africa. Its root bark is used by the Bwiti tribe for ritual, ceremony, and healing on every level. Like other plant medicines it's used for psycho-spiritual purposes, but it also has the incredible ability to heal strong addictions. It has an amazing track record of curing opiate addiction quickly and with minimal withdrawal symptoms as long as the recipient is ready to do the work. (Seeking a trained Iboga detox provider or going to an Ibogaine Clinic is necessary when addressing addictions with this medicine). When I went into my first ceremony, I was interested in the psycho-spiritual effects of Iboga and was specifically interested in learning about how my mind works and how I can make better use of it.

One of Iboga's specialties is the mind. It teaches us how our mind functions so that we can learn to use it for our own happiness instead of letting it use us. With this intention in my heart, I took the medicine, and since Iboga has a reputation for being one of the strongest psychedelic substances on the planet, I was pretty nervous. However, as the medicine began to take effect in my body, I immediately felt its powerful and loving energy wash over me. I knew without a doubt that I was safe and in good hands.

Throughout the night, Iboga fully delivered my intention to me. I learned so much about myself and how the mind works. I was shown how to consciously choose each thought and how to change my mind's default mechanism. I could see that my default mechanism was fear and how consciously choosing a different thought over and over again, changes that default response. It showed me how to clear my mind and how to keep it clear. Iboga not only delivered my desire to understand my mind, it over-delivered in many other ways. I was shown numerous things that I had locked away—things that I knew were true but didn't want to believe.

Iboga has a way of showing us these deep uncomfortable things from a completely detached place so that we can observe them without being overwhelmed by the emotion of the experience. The medicine found these hidden traumas for me and brought them to the surface as if to say, "See you were right, why do you doubt yourself?" These repressed childhood memories were presented to me in a very simple and matter-of-fact way which opened the door for the healing of these traumas. By accepting what had happened in a detached and non-personal way, I was able to disconnect from the events and see that they were not a part of who I am, they were merely something that happened in my life. Over the next year following my Iboga ceremonies, I dove into the challenging work of healing these deep traumas and I felt the Iboga medicine with me, guiding me and supporting me every step of the way.

I am deeply grateful for all of my plant medicine experiences and my relationships with these powerful allies. They catapulted my healing process and kept me from tip-toeing around things that I had been trying to avoid.

Over the past 10 years or so, sacred and ancient plant medicines have become more accessible and more sought after. I believe that both of these things are strong indicators that we as humans are ready to go deeper into our healing and spiritual transformation. However, we must approach all of these powerful plants with deep respect.

Besides Ayahuasca and Iboga, there are many other sacred medicines that can be used for our spiritual growth and healing. These include (but are not limited to) San Pedro, Peyote, Bufo, Kambo, and Psilocybin mushrooms. If you are feeling called to work with any of these medicines, please do your research. Do not work with these medicines on your own. Find a provider who has lots of experience, proper training, a good reputation, deep respect for the medicine, knows how to hold space, and is someone who you feel a connection with. Finding the right situation and provider is just as important as the medicine itself.

Also, keep in mind that the plant medicine experience is just the beginning. The real work continues after the ceremony is over. Taking time to complete any healing processes that were sparked during the ceremony and fully integrating the experience into your everyday life is essential to getting the most out of these powerful peak moments. If you are new to these medicines, be sure to seek out and line up support for your post-ceremony integration process.

Meditation, Breathwork, Yoga, and Sound Healing

Plant medicine is a powerful tool. However, it's not for everyone. If you don't feel called to work with these powerful psychedelics and conscious-altering substances, don't worry, there are many other transformative tools available.

The most accessible and least expensive tool we can access is **meditation**. Meditation is the practice of being still, being fully present with yourself, and quieting the mind. It's an unfolding practice, not a goal. The benefits come from the practice itself, there's no finish line.

When I first heard about meditation in my early 20s, it sounded like a magic bullet. I thought, *Cool, I'll just sit down under this tree, focus on my breathing and all of my anxiety and troubles will disappear.* Ha! That couldn't have been farther from the truth. As soon as I sat down and focused on my breathing, my mind did NOT get quieter. It got MUCH louder. This was due to the fact it was the first time that I had actually taken the time to slow down and notice my mind—and I was in for a big surprise!

Needless to say, I didn't last very long under that tree. I got up feeling very discouraged and I let go of the idea of meditation for a while. However, down the road, I learned that there are many different types of meditation. At some point, I found a meditation in a book that had a specific step-by-step process on how to build and strengthen my energy field. The individual steps gave my monkey mind something to focus on and connected the experience back to my body—I was not stuck in my mind. Using this meditation daily, helped me to understand the benefits of meditation while also giving me a structure for being able to observe my mind without being carried away with it.

There are countless forms of meditation. Finding the one that works best for you, dropping your expectations, and beginning with curiosity, is a great place to start. Some of the different forms of meditation include guided meditation, instructional meditation, mindfulness meditation, vipassana meditation, transcendental meditation, and movement meditation.

Guided meditations are a great starting point. Simply find a recorded meditation that appeals to you, close your eyes, and follow along with the prompting of the speaker.

Instructional meditation is the type of meditation that I described above. It gives step-by-step instructions to follow, that lead you into a meditative state and may have a secondary purpose such as healing, clearing, or strengthening the body and energy field.

Mindfulness meditation is about bringing awareness to your thoughts and feelings. It combines deep breathing with the witness perspective—watching the mind from a place of non-attachment.

Vipassana meditation, also known as Insight meditation, is one of the oldest Buddhist meditation practices. It is typically the meditation practice that is used during a silent meditation retreat.

Transcendental meditation is an ancient Vedic technique that utilizes mantras to transcend the limitations of the mind. It's designed to be effortless and relaxing.

Movement meditation uses repetitive movement to evoke a meditative state. Walking, dancing, and running can all be used as a form of movement meditation.

Breathwork is another powerful practice that is similar to meditation but also involves a very physical action and bodily response. Our breath is our lifeline and it sets the rhythm for our life.

Each inhale feeds our body with oxygen and connects us with the world around us. Each exhale clears the body of carbon dioxide and helps us release old energy. Breathing is automatic. We don't have to think about it. Unfortunately, that means that our breathing is often the first thing that is compromised when we start to experience stress, anxiety, and fear. Our breath becomes shallow. This does not just happen while we're experiencing stress. Most people habitually breathe in a very shallow way which taxes the nervous system, creates more anxiety, and deprives the body of oxygen. When we practice breathing techniques we can change these harmful breathing habits and teach ourselves to breathe deeply again.

There are many types of breathing practices. Some focus on the inhale which calms the nervous system and brings more oxygen into the body. Some focus on the exhale which helps to clear the body of unwanted energy and stimulates the various systems of the body. Some focus on an even inhale and exhale to create heart/brain coherence and balance the body. There are shorter practices that are easily done alone and there are longer practices that require having a trained breathwork practitioner who can lead you through the practice and hold space for you as you transform yourself with your breath. Both types of practices can bring up latent energies, trigger awakening experiences, and create deep healing in the body.

If you're interested in developing a breathwork practice, do some research and find the type of breathwork that speaks to you. Just like guided meditations, short guided breathwork practices are a great place to start. For a deeper and more personal experience, find a trained breathwork practitioner to assist you on your breathing journey.

Yoga is another powerful tool that is becoming increasingly popular and is also very accessible. Yoga is an ancient system of well-being, originating in India that combines meditation, breathing, movement, and physical postures. There are so many forms of yoga. Some forms focus more on the physical aspects, some focus more on breath, and some focus more on spiritual transformation and the opening of energy channels in the body. However, all of these forms are created to bring balance to the whole being—mind, body, and soul.

I've had countless students who have had awakening experiences during a yoga class or while doing their yoga practice at home. These experiences were triggered by various forms of yoga and different practices. Any form of yoga could possibly spark the awakening process in an open individual. However, kundalini yoga is the style of yoga that is most commonly associated with spiritual awakening. It is an ancient practice that is designed to prepare the body for the activation and flow of kundalini energy, moving from the base of the spine, up through the chakras and through the entire body.

A kundalini awakening is a spiritual awakening but not all spiritual awakenings are full kundalini awakenings. Since a kundalini awakening IS a spiritual awakening, the symptoms and stages are the same.

Practicing kundalini yoga can help to prepare and support the body for the massive changes that occur during the awakening process. Just like all of the other tools, if you are interested in exploring kundalini yoga or any type of yoga, be sure to do your research and find an experienced, well-trained teacher with a good reputation.

One of my biggest passions in life is **sound healing.** I've been using sound with my private clients, in groups, and in classes for about 10 years. Sound healing, like the other tools I've shared has become increasingly popular and much more accessible. Scientific studies are also beginning to validate the efficacy of sound healing.

Sound healing is based on the fact that everything in the Universe is in vibration. Not only is it IN vibration but it IS vibration. If we were no longer vibrating, we would cease to exist. Because of this, we each have our own resonant frequency. Each organ and cell of our body has its own innate frequency and together they create our inner symphony. When we are sick, injured, stressed, or depressed, part of our physiology has gone out of tune. We are no longer vibrating at our resonant frequency of health, wholeness, and balance. Additionally, when we are disconnected from ourselves, when we have experienced the original heartbreak, swallowed the lies, and believed the illusions, we are also out of tune with ourselves.

Sound healing is the process of bringing ourselves back into harmony, tuning our bodies so they can function at their highest potential, and clearing the dissonant frequencies so that we can hear the song of our soul once again. Sound healing journeys have the ability to induce altered states of consciousness, awakening experiences, and deep meditative states. They may also calm the nervous system, relieve stress and pain, and spark spontaneous healing.

There are many types of sound healing and each sound healer has their own unique style and their own collection of instruments that they use. Some of the instruments I use are planetary tuning forks, gongs, crystal and Tibetan singing bowls, drums, chimes, bells, and a monochord instrument. The voice in the form of singing, chanting, or light language, can also be a potent sound healing tool. Additionally, these tools are great for self-care and can be incorporated into your meditation or breathwork practice.

Sound healing recordings can be found online and can definitely be an easy and effective form. It's a great place to start. However, for the full sound healing experience you need to physically feel the vibrations of these powerful instruments as they move through your body. Having an in-person private session or group sound bath experience is highly recommended.

There are countless other tools that can be extremely helpful in the awakening process. Practices like tai chi, chi gong, reiki, and other energy work modalities are amazing options. Follow your heart. Explore the possibilities and let your heart lead you to the tools that will be the most beneficial to where you are right now.

Shadow Work

"One does not become enlightened
by imagining figures of light,
but by making the darkness conscious."
Carl Jung

There are parts of all of us that we have disowned, turned our back on, and pushed away—experiences, personality traits, things we've done, mistakes we've made, or parts of ourselves that we are ashamed of or afraid of. These pieces of us get relegated to the depths of our subconscious. We lock them away and avoid them at all costs. These parts of us create our shadow self. Healing, loving, and integrating those parts of the self is what we call shadow work and it is an absolutely necessary part of spiritual transformation. It is also one of the most challenging and uncomfortable aspects of awakening.

Shadow work is a term that has become a popular spiritual buzzword. Oftentimes my clients will hear this word and come to me and say "I need to do shadow work. Can you do shadow work with me?" My response is always that they are already doing it. If they are working with me, they are doing shadow work. If you are facing the parts of yourself that you have kept hidden, denied, and disliked, you are doing shadow work. Awakening, at its core, IS shadow work.

A physical shadow cannot be seen in complete darkness. A bit of light is needed to see that shadow and as the light increases so does the shadow—until the light is bright enough to consume the shadow completely.

The same is true for the awakening process. Awakening is the light that illuminates the darkness. It brings the shadow self to the surface. The hidden becomes seen and once it is seen it can not be unseen. As our light gets brighter, so does the shadow until our awareness, acceptance, and light are bright enough to consume that aspect of our shadow self.

To do shadow work we must be willing to be brutally honest with ourselves. To see where your shadow work lies, become aware of your triggers. Notice what throws you off and evokes unreasonable emotional reactions. This will show you what you have been avoiding.

It takes courage to face these parts of ourselves that we have been hiding from for so long. It often feels like our shadows will consume us if we face them but we have to remember that it is our light and our love that will consume the shadow. It is also important, while doing this work, to stay out of judgment. Our judgment is just another shadow aspect so it will only make the shadow grow. Whatever hidden parts of yourself that you have uncovered just want what everyone and everything else wants—to be seen, accepted, and loved.

It can be helpful and often necessary to have help and support while facing our shadows. We may need someone else to hold space for us so that we can feel safe enough to lean into this work. Finding someone who is experienced and skilled to walk with you through this process can make all the difference. They can help you to see in the dark.

Journaling is also a very helpful tool to help bring the darkness to light. Writing can be a cathartic and meditative practice that helps you tap into your subconscious.

Grab your journal and try this:

1. identify and list the parts of yourself that you are avoiding, ashamed of, or hiding from.

2. Tell the origin story of that part of yourself. Where did it come from, how was it formed and when did you lock it away?

3. Have a conversation with that part of yourself. Listen to what it has to teach you. Talk to it.

4. Bring it back in, welcome it home, and give it your unconditional love.

Like awakening, shadow work is not a one-and-done thing. It is not something that we can check off the list. Our shadow surfaces in layers over time. It is often when we think we are done with this work, that another aspect of the shadow appears. Be curious, be vigilant, and continue to build your self-awareness. As you do this, the shadow work becomes easier and easier. Self-love and acceptance become your new default mode.

Self Care Is Not Selfish

There is an old, deep, often subconscious, collective belief that in order to be a good person or a spiritual person, we must be completely selfless, put others first, and put our needs last. We've even been taught that loving ourselves and taking good care of ourselves is the product of an over-inflated ego. We've been taught that it's selfish, but nothing could be further from the truth. Putting ourselves last, and catering to everyone else's needs first, is actually the product of the ego. It comes from the limiting beliefs that we adopt after we experience the original heartbreak and shift our power center from heart to head.

These limiting beliefs may sound something like this:

- "I'm not worthy of having my needs taken care of."

- "I'm not worthy of taking care of myself."

- "Other people are better than me and more important than me."

- "I have to take care of others to prove my worthiness."

- "I have to help others so that they will like me and not reject me."

These beliefs are often deeply subconscious. We may not even know they are there until we start exploring our resistance to taking care of ourselves or loving ourselves. Awakening has a brilliant way of bringing these beliefs to the surface. Once we begin to see the truth and beauty of who we actually are, we can no longer accept these beliefs as truth.

As we reconnect with ourselves, we naturally want to take better care of ourselves. As we go through the intense symptoms of awakening, we often quickly learn that we have no choice but to take care of ourselves. Since awakening is a shifting of all of the parts of us, it affects every system of the body—especially the nervous system. Nurturing the nervous system with more rest, more sleep, eating nutrient-rich foods, and light exercise, is a great place to start. We often find that we absolutely need more sleep, we crave a healthier diet and we no longer want to participate in self-destructive habits.

In addition to the basics of self-care, it is also extremely helpful to create a daily self-care routine that includes practices like meditation, yoga, breathwork, or journaling. Having a daily practice not only helps to mitigate the intense awakening symptoms, it also gives you a space to work through the issues and emotions that are coming to the surface. This will help you to move through the transformational process more quickly and more gracefully.

I have found for myself that my daily morning practice of meditation, breathwork, and prayer through gratitude is a non-negotiable part of my day. As the collective awakening process speeds up and life intensifies, these daily practices are essential for maintaining a clear and healthy vibration, a healthy nervous system and mental state, and being available to show up for the work we came here to do. When we are depleted, we have nothing left to share with our family, friends, community, co-workers, or clients. Not only that, we may also hurt the people we love without meaning to, simply because we are too exhausted. Making self-care a priority is not selfish at all. It benefits everyone we come into contact with and, by example, it gives them permission to take care of themselves as well.

Self-care can be a radical act of self-love. Take the time to curate the daily self-care practices that are best for your body, mind, and soul. We all have different needs and respond differently to various practices. What works for someone else may not necessarily work for you. Be kind to yourself and know that this is not homework. It is an act of deep kindness and compassion for yourself.

Your Path Is the Right Path

There is no right or wrong way to go through the awakening process. It's a mapless road, a "choose your own adventure." We must find our own way through it, and forge our own path.

We all come from different cultures, different backgrounds, and different experiences. We have different levels of resources available to us but the beauty of the awakening process is that none of this matters at all. It's an organic force of the universe that moves through us when we are ready. We do not need to work with plant medicine, do yoga, or even meditate. The process can happen on its own. What we do need to have is the courage to keep going, to find support when we need it, and to not give up on ourselves.

Trust that it is unfolding exactly as it needs to for your deepest healing and highest good. The energy of awakening comes from the energy of life itself in its purest form. This energy is pure love—it can be nothing less. Trust the process. Follow your path as it unfolds before you and know that you are being guided, supported, and held with love, every step of the way.

When the mind falls away,
When you see that you are so much more than
you ever "thought,"
The truth of this Universe and who you really are
begins to flood in.
It doesn't come in words, thoughts, or ideas.
It comes as a feeling, a knowing, a whisper.
It comes as Love.

Chapter 8

Rebirth

Dreaming a New Dream

As I begin writing this last chapter, I find myself sitting in a sweet little cafe in Mount Shasta, California, staring out the window at the mountain. My mind is empty, no words are coming, but I'm filled with endless gratitude. I'm overwhelmed with awe for this crazy, beautiful world that we all chose to live in at this moment in time.

Though the chaos and intensity of our human existence seem to be building every day, I'm filled with hope. I know this cycle. Chaos to form. Contraction to expansion. Inner struggle to inner peace. Destruction to creation. Death to rebirth. It can be no other way. This is the process of awakening—to experience these cycles over and over again, spiraling inward until we are seated so deeply into our soul, into our truth, and into our hearts, once again.

As we complete this spiraling and drop back into the center of our being, something interesting happens. The spiral reverses and we begin to move outward again. However, this time, because we are now deeply rooted in ourselves, this outward movement feels different—vulnerable but safe, scary but exciting at the same time. It feels exhilarating but also a bit intimidating to begin to move back out into the world in a whole new way.

As we spiral outward our rebirth begins. We begin to be shown and to show who we really are. This rebirth can feel awkward at first—like a baby fawn tripping over its own feet as it finds its footing. This time, we are no longer guided by and moving from our ego. We have to learn to walk all over again. This time, the movement, the motivation, and the vision come from our heart and are deeply rooted in our soul, so it feels different. This new way of living and moving may feel foreign when we try to relate to it from the level of the mind but when we relate to it from the deep personal, inner level of the heart, it feels like home, familiar and cozy.

Just as we are going through these cycles of death and rebirth, the planet also is experiencing these same cycles for the same purpose—complete transformation.

Personal Rebirth—Living from Love and Authenticity

As individuals, when we begin to spiral out and find our footing, we also find a new strength and a deepening clarity. This is where we learn to live from our truth and authenticity, which is not something we do but something we lean into, something we embrace, something that flows out of us as we allow it to lead us forward. This shift from ego to authenticity opens up and expands us into a whole new realm of possibility.

Since the ego-centered self is the small self, we have been playing small our whole lives, until now. As we open to a bigger truth, we are opening to a bigger self—the eternal, expansive, authentic self that is pure spirit and has no boundaries or limitations. Once we strip away the illusions of the ego we begin to feel the authentic self emerging. What's been underneath the layers of pain, programming, and trauma can now be revealed. What that is exactly, is very difficult to talk about because who we are cannot be put into words. The truth cannot be put into words, it can only be seen, felt, and experienced. We are so much bigger than our small minds can conceive.

However, when we connect with the truth of who we are, we find that the life that once felt very limited and threatening is really a wide open field of possibility, support, and pure love. This is what it means to live authentically and it is a product of heart-centered living. When we are led by our hearts and our souls, we will speak with truth and power, we will have compassion for others, and everything we choose to do will be infused with the energy of pure authenticity. However, we must remember that authenticity is not stagnant. It's not an end goal or an accomplishment, it's a way of life. How we live authentically is always changing because WE are always changing, always growing, and always evolving.

Living authentically from the heart is about following the thread of our interests and curiosities. It's about living with awareness instead of living with a step-by-step plan and a list of requirements or responsibilities.

As we listen to our inner guidance system and follow the signs and suggestions from the universe, we will be led to the places, people, and experiences that we need. I never imagined that I would be writing this book, helping people through this process or doing sound healing events for hundreds of people, but I've been following the thread, the voice of my soul and it has led me here.

Before we awakened we were dreaming—but we didn't know that we were dreaming and therefore we had no conscious choice in how the dream unfolded. Now that we have awakened—we are still dreaming in the sense that we are creating and moving through this momentary existence, but now we are doing so consciously. We are now aware of the dream so we get to dream a new dream.

As we reclaim our power of choice and awareness we are no longer victims of life- we are the creators. This is lucid living, dreaming while awake. As each one of us begins to choose a life that is lived with authenticity, compassion, and love, we will not only change our own lives, we will change the world.

As you begin your spiral back out into the world, being reborn in your authentic form, take some time to find your footing. Get used to how it feels to be guided by your heart and follow the thread of your love. Follow the thread of the universe and know that you will be guided, supported, and held in love every step of the way.

Planetary Rebirth—The Collective Uprising

The incredible thing about awakening is that it works the same on the planetary level as it does on the personal level. Planetary awakening mirrors personal awakening and personal awakening mirrors planetary awakening. The two are deeply intertwined. We are a microcosm of the macrocosm—a reflection, a hologram.

This is why our personal awakening process is so important—because it directly affects the awakening of our planet. Likewise, as the planet awakens, the energy is shifting, the vibration is rising, the wave is building and more and more people are waking up, transforming, and healing. It's an exciting time to be alive!

It's mind-blowing to watch the planet going through these stages of the awakening process. Collectively, we have had endless wake-up calls, dark nights of the soul, time in the void, and times of rebirth as we move through cycle after cycle of spiritual evolution. Like our own awakening process, it's not always pretty and it doesn't always look like an awakening at first. Just as all of our own trauma, pain, conditioning, and toxicity have to come to the surface in order to be healed and cleared to make room for something new, it's the same for the planet.

Right now on this Earth, we are going through a massive purging and clearing process. As the vibration of the Earth rises, nothing can hide any longer. All of the ugliness is coming to the surface in order to be seen and cleared and in order to make room for a new reality, a new paradigm. Just like our own egos choose to throw a fit during this process, the collective ego is also fighting back, kicking and screaming, and trying to sweep it all back under the rug. But it's not going to fit. The death of the old is already in motion and the birth of the new Earth has begun.

I know this may seem naive, unrealistic, or overly optimistic given the state of the world, but that is only if we are observing the world from the mind or from a place of fear. As more and more humans awaken, this perception is changing. Many of us are beginning to observe from the heart and from a much more expansive place of love and possibility. The simple act of changing how we observe the world has the potential to change the outcome. It changes what we are observing. In order to change how we perceive the world we must first change ourselves, heal ourselves, and love ourselves. This is what is happening right now through our personal and collective awakening, and it is breathtakingly beautiful.

Rising in Love, Rising Together

The process of spiritual awakening leads us directly to deep, unconditional self-love. It's a by-product of all of the grueling personal work and healing that we've done. Trying to love ourselves can feel impossible when we are in the throes of the transformation process but once we have come out the other side we often come to the realization, "Oh, this is what self-love feels like!"

Loving ourselves is not an act of ego. It's an act of incredible courage and strength. To fall in love with ourselves we have to look at all of the ways that we have hurt, damaged, and disrespected ourselves. It's not for the faint of heart and it truly is a fall. We fall to our knees.

We surrender our ego and we fall deeper and deeper into ourselves with each act of self-acceptance and self-forgiveness. We fall so deeply into ourselves that we can finally see the truth of who and what we really are.

It's at this point when we can truly love ourselves that we will be able to love others. Once we glimpse the truth of our eternal, expansive, limitless self, we will begin to see it in others. When we accept that at our very core, we are pure spirit and that we are made from and will return to the highest source of infinite love, then we must admit that the same is true for each and every other soul on this planet. This can be hard to accept with the mind so give it to the heart.

As we are able to find love, acceptance, and compassion for ourselves we are then able to slowly extend that same energy to the people around us. This is the new Earth being birthed through each act of self-love, each act of kindness and compassion, and each time we choose something better the morphic field of love and acceptance is rippling outward like a pebble in a pond.

We are falling in love with ourselves so that we can rise in love together. It's happening in every corner of the world. It is a powerful, unconquerable force of nature that will heal our planet and you are a vital part of this unfolding.

So, thank you for doing the work. Thank you for standing in the fires. Thank you for not shying away from the pain. Thank you for being present in the midst of destruction. You are powerful, you are beautiful, you are perfect and you are whole. I love you.

Acknowledgments

With endless gratitude...

There are so many amazing people who contributed to the creation of this book. Without them, this manuscript never would have seen the light of day.

First and foremost, to each and every one of my students and clients who trusted me through their deeply personal process of transformation, dying and being reborn. Your courage, wisdom and strength have taught me so much.

To my daughters Sequoia and Freya who have been my biggest teachers and my greatest inspiration for healing myself, facing my shadow, and being the best possible version of me that I can be. You never stop inspiring me.

To my beloved partner Paul for seeing me, encouraging me, and standing beside me through all of the highs and lows of creating and publishing a book.

To my first clients (and now friends), Chris V. who planted the seeds of this book and harassed me until I began to write it, and Katy H.P. for helping me to find my voice and my footing as I began this process.

To all of my incredible friends who listened to me, encouraged me, and were my first readers. Your love and support means more than you can know.

To Elizabeth Hill of Green Heart Living Press for skillfully walking me through the publishing process and helping me to turn my dream into reality.

To all of my teachers, mentors, angels, guides and ancestors, seen and unseen, who have guided me through this life and led me to all of the adventures and opportunities that have gotten me to this perfect moment right here.

And finally, to everyone on this planet who is currently moving through the beautiful, challenging and potent process of awakening. Together we are tipping the scales. Together we ARE creating a new Earth.

Thank you, thank you, thank you...

Resources

Awakening, Transformation & Healing

www.jenmadrone.com
YouTube: Jen Madrone
Instagram: @dreamingourselvesawake
FB group: Dreaming Ourselves Awake

Sound Healing

Inner Alchemy Healing and Sound
www.jenmadrone/soundhealing.com
Instagram: @inneralchemyhealingandsound

West Coast Acutonics
www.westcoastacutonics.com

Plant Medicine

Iboga
Iboga Rebirth
Instagram: @iboga.rebirth
www.ibogarebirth.com

Root Healing
Instagram: @root_healing_iboga
www.roothealing.com

Muanga Benda Missoko Bwiti Church
www.muangabenda.com

Ayahuasca
Fen Meadow Retreat Center
Email: michael@touchofthewild.net

Nihue Rao Peru
Instagram: @Nihuerao
www.nihuerao.org

About the Author

Jen Madrone lives in the Pacific Northwest between the redwoods and the sea. She's a spiritual teacher, sound healer, reiki master, bodyworker, and teacher of the healing arts. She has been guiding others through the processes of healing and transformation for over 20 years.

She has cultivated a large online community of like-minded awakening humans with a comprehensive library of videos on YouTube to assist in the awakening process. She also loves to support her local community with group sound healing events, gong baths on the beach, and various classes and retreats.

Through the years Jen's work has been deeply influenced by her love and extensive studies of indigenous healing, mysticism, plant medicine, energy, vibration, and the mysteries of nature. When she's not writing or playing her gongs she can probably be found wandering somewhere through the forest.

www.jenmadrone.com

Printed in Great Britain
by Amazon

52816567R00099